DUNCAN NORTON-TAYLOR

WITH MY HEART IN MY MOUTH

COWARD-McCANN, INC., NEW YORK

MANUFACTURED IN THE UNITED STATES OF AMERICA
Van Rees Press, New York

Second Impression

To
PEG

"TULAGI SECURED"

THE DUST JACKET is from a painting by Lieutenant Dwight Shepler, U.S.N.R., entitled "Tulagi Secured." Lieutenant Shepler is one of five officer-artists commissioned by the Navy to record its World War II campaigns with on-the-scene paintings. Lieutenant Shepler was born in Everett, Massachusetts, is thirty-eight years old, has exhibited at the Chicago Art Institute, the Pennsylvania Academy of Fine Arts and the Boston Museum of Fine Arts. As an amateur blue-water sailor he cruised the East Coast, the waters of Ecuador, the Galapagos, Guatanamo. As a Navy officer-artist he was under fire during the Battle of Santa Cruz, spent three weeks on Guadalcanal during the struggle for the island in the fall of 1942 and has covered all of the area described in *With My Heart in My Mouth*.

CONTENTS

WITH MY HEART IN MY MOUTH

I

ASSIGNMENT: PACIFIC

It was the moment we dreaded. Peg and the children had been to the opera that afternoon. We met afterwards, had supper at a decorous tea room and walked to the airline office on Forty-second Street. In the raw chill of the April evening we rode out in the limousine to La Guardia Field, got out and followed a dim corridor to Gate 6. There we clustered. The children looked tired and suddenly stopped talking. Their father had been away before but he had never been 9000 miles away on a battlefront. Peg and I tried to think of the important, absolutely final things to say. "Take care of yourself." We said good-bye.

The curtains of the plane were drawn according to wartime regulations but I pulled one corner aside to look back and see their four smudged figures behind the dirty window at Gate 6. The plane roared across the field. One thing about farewells at airfields, they are abrupt. There is no interminable waving and waving of hands, like the slow unraveling of strands. The break is sudden and sharp and that's the end of it.

I tried to read. We came down on a windswept field at Philadelphia, where I got out to stretch, turning up the collar of my trench coat. A man who disembarked was met by a little girl. She said she had never seen the inside of an airliner and he told her he thought he had left his glasses aboard and for her to run back and ask the stewardess. She ran and stood inside the door, staring and stammering, until the man laughed and called out that he had found his glasses after all and waved her back. A half-dozen ferry pilots got aboard and we took off again into the dark overcast. From the conversation I guessed that the pilots ferried P-38's and were headed for some dispersal base in the South. Though they looked too young to be either very wise or very professional they had a wise, professional air. At Washington, women in slacks gave a hand to the unloading and loading, darted around the airport in electric trucks. At Nashville it was a woman's voice that came drawling out over the public address system. I slept a little after that. But sleeping was fitful. With me were the recollection of the four figures behind the window at Gate 6 and the disquieting thought of where I was going.

There had been a long prelude to that April night, when I might have reconsidered and turned the trip down. There were others who had wanted the assignment. Having accepted I had begun to have doubts. I would miss Peg and her conscientious care. I would miss the routine comforts. I would not be happy surrounded by the violence of war. I even began to have moments of dark premonition.

Whit Chambers, who was convalescing on his Maryland farm from serious illness, had written: "You must want to see action and from the way the Japs are shuttling back and forth between the interior bases and the outward islands I believe you have a better than good chance to see something. I'll think of you many times out there and will wish you well. It will be a great experience for you to watch the future of the world determined there...."

We came down in Memphis. Rain lashed against the windows of the plane as we took off again, the sound of it seeming to accelerate our onrush.

I had a curiously guilty feeling about my luck. I had been too young to fight in the last war, too old to be drafted into this one—one of the in-between, slacktide generation. I felt conscience-stricken over such luck.

"Since I was a youth I've known in the broad outlines just about what the history of our times was going to be like," Whit had written from his sickbed. "I even thought it rather enjoyable to watch history in the intimate making until one day I opened my eyes and saw that it was horror. In the last three months I've crammed history—from early Egypt to Franklin Roosevelt. All I've learned, it seems to me, is that the plot is always the same and the play is always bad. The last acts have

4

been especially bad. Lunatics would love them. But I observe the people felt the same way in the last centuries B.C.

"The nearer you sit to the exit the less you can be impressed by the murder in Act IV and the more you are amused by the way the actors forget their lines and cues, the way they rant and roar. Have a good time and memorable trip but above all a safe homecoming."

I was insured. When I left the country as an overseas correspondent the firm would take out $25,000 more insurance for me so Peg and the three children were protected somewhat.

It would have taken a certain courage to turn the assignment down and that courage I didn't possess.

There had been a long delay while I waited for my orders from the Navy. Cowpox, typhoid, typhus, tetanus, yellow fever, cholera inoculations laid me low. Washington interviewed and fingerprinted me, although the FBI had already investigated my past. I was expensively outfitted by the firm with Army khakis, a large canvas kitbag, a trench coat. I got a War Department identification card and a letter of accreditation to the Pacific Fleet. I laid in an extra pair of spectacles, I went to the dentist for a last check-up, and at last the orders came. I was to report at once in San Francisco.

I had bought a one-way ticket to New York that morning. The ticket agent seemed surprised. Commuters always returned to our suburban town with its pretty park and its pretty municipal building and its high tax rate. "A one-way ticket," I said, and when the train came I lifted my kitbag, a zipper bag and a brief case aboard. I had a sense of the finality of things that morning, though I unfolded my *New York Times* exactly as I did every morning on my way to New York. I thought of H. M. Tomlinson riding to a destination in the jungles on the 8:35. But Tomlinson, not knowing then where his train was going to cast him, brooding over his frostbitten dahlias, viewed the familiar scenes with rebellion. I looked at them with the alarming thought that it might be for the last time. There was a stretch of factory buildings. As a boy, sitting with my nose squashed against the window of a gas-lit D. L. & W. coach (the "Road of Anthracite") on pilgrimages with my parents to the New York Hippodrome, I used to look at

5

tall brick factory chimneys and feel stirred. This was the great world and it was almost as thrilling as the Hippodrome itself, where girls dived from the roof and the whole cast of characters finally vanished into a tank of water on the stage. There was one chimney which bore the legend: "No-Name Hat Mfg. Co.," which always mystified me. It was gone now; the Hippodrome had vanished into a heap of rubble; Anthracite had given way to Electrification. I sat staring out the window as the train hummed through Newark, over the Passaic and Hackensack Rivers and into the dirty, familiar train shed at Hoboken. . . .

Rain continued to beat against the windows of the transcontinental plane. We were flying by the southern route and were due to reach San Francisco the next day.

Dawn broke through the overcast above Arkansas and there were occasional glimpses of flatlands, rivers in oxbow bends and flooded fields. "We may be weathered in for two-three days," one of the ferry pilots said. Rain-heavy clouds closed around us and held us until we came out over northeast Texas. We came down briefly in Dallas, where for the first time I had a warm, wet whiff of the year's tardy spring.

Brown earth and fresh green fields, brown earth and spiraling plow-patterns, mesas, gulches, the bright dot of a tin roof, the desert, Phoenix, crumpled foothills, the snow-topped Bernardinos, the Salton Sea, sun-drenched Desert Airport, Imperial Valley, Los Angeles. . . . On my way to the South Pacific I was seeing the southwestern states for the first time. Months later in Sydney, Australia, called upon to sing what amounted to a solo rendition of the National Anthem, mellow with wine from a number of toasts, I recollected that single glimpse of southwestern America and felt homesick for it.

Bob deRoos, our man in San Francisco, had managed to get me a reservation at the St. Francis Hotel and it was lucky that he had, because what I had supposed would be just a few hours to embarkation turned out to be days. I checked in at the 12th Naval District headquarters off Market Street, presented my credentials, and waited. I learned later that the greater part of a war correspondent's job is waiting for something or other and developed more patience. San Francisco was crowded and the St. Francis Hotel was the center of the wartime excitement.

6

Every officer westward or eastward bound sooner or later must have passed through the big, ornate lobby. The sidewalk on Powell Street was cluttered with foot-lockers, leather and canvas kitbags, barracks bags. Dining room and cocktail lounge were filled with a feverish, last-fling atmosphere, crowded with officers of the Pacific Fleet on furlough, Marines, artillerymen, Air Corps men, ferry pilots, Australians, New Zealanders, Waves, Wacs, Army and Navy nurses and pretty girls. It was a rendezvous and a place of assignation. The lobby doors spun and spun.

I went to see Boris Karloff in *Arsenic and Old Lace*. I checked over my gear and made sorties for extra supplies which I figured I might need, vital matériel ranging from dental floss to half a dozen bottles of Bourbon. I took the Powell Street cable car up to the Mark Hopkins Hotel and watched the sunset from the roof. I was interested in the Chinese language and had studied it sporadically that winter. Now with an unknown amount of time on my hands I decided to put in a few licks at it and looked up a Chinese teacher. There are plenty of Cantonese in San Francisco but not so many Chinese who speak pure and official Mandarin. I finally found a Mrs. Lee and in Mrs. Lee's apartment on Mason Street chanted in *Kuo Yü* (the National Language): "The man does not have calves and lambs . . . The man does not see the huge mountains . . . Are dogs men? No, dogs are not men," while Mrs. Lee listened stoically, trying to correct my mispronunciations. It is a subtle language. The most delicate intonations make the difference between life and death.

Mrs. Lee's four-year-old daughter hovered beside us, gazing at me with childish wonder. I asked Mrs. Lee if her daughter spoke Chinese. Mrs. Lee said primly: "She speaks the purest Mandarin."

I read on, trying to give such questions as "Whose is the little dog outside the main gate?" a portentousness too deep for a four-year-old *hai tzu*. She had planted herself at my elbow. Occasionally I shot a glance at her little, round blossom of a face. "Men are not cows," I labored on. "*Jen pu niu.*" "Men also are not sheep." It came time to go. Mrs. Lee's daughter said suddenly and brightly: "Happy Easter!"

7

"Does she speak English too?"

Mrs. Lee said primly: "Yes, she speaks perfect English."

We Americans are a dull race, by and large, I reflected. But some of my self-esteem was restored several days later when I found Mrs. Lee's little *hai tzu* wolfing jelly beans out of an Easter basket and I told myself smugly, She's in for a bad time. There is a lot more to be learned in this world than how to speak perfect English and *Kuo Yü.*

I took a long walk that afternoon around Telegraph Hill. I was tired and very hungry when I got back to the hotel. With anticipation I ordered a *daiquiri,* a dish of creamed crabmeat and some fresh asparagus. But suddenly, before I got to coffee and dessert, I was seized with a strange lassitude. I walked out dizzily and had just reached the crowded corridor on the way to the elevator bank when my legs gave way and I collapsed. I came to before anyone had a chance to help me and pulled myself over to the cigar counter, where I hung on, breathing heavily. A naval lieutenant looked at me curiously. He asked if he could give me a hand and half dragged me into an elevator and up to my room. I sank on the bed and he called the house nurse. She was baffled until I told her what I had eaten. She grunted and propped my legs up on a couple of pillows. She had what amounted to an obsession against rich, creamed food, she said. She was very stern. She said that the blood had all rushed to my stomach. Propping my legs up would start it circulating again. She ordered me some brandy. The next time that I was tired and hungry I should show a little discretion and eat something simple.

I met the water-colorist Dong Kingman, a little Chinese in a tweed jacket and a cocky soft hat. He told me that he was born thirty-two years before in Oakland but at the age of five was transported back to China by his father, who ran a dry goods store in Hong Kong. There Dong studied under painters who taught him the classic, pattern-like Chinese style, which he discarded when he returned to the United States. Dong— Dong is a romanization of his family name, Kingman of his given name—adapted his art to Western styles because he wanted to be understood. "All I want is a Chinaman's chance," he laughed. He was getting better than an average Chinaman's chance, having received a second well-deserved Guggenheim Fellowship. He had won an award at the Chicago International Water-color Exhibition, and art institutes and galleries were buying his work. His paintings of America bespeak China's hopes for her own future.

His home was in San Francisco with his two small sons and his pretty Chinese wife. But a good part of his time Mr. Kingman spent running around the United States, peering at its wonders and painting them with a knowing and appreciative eye. He paints with terrific color and unexpected drollery. Into his lovely, splashed scenes he is apt to drop a piece of impish humor like the little sign which appears in a corner of his "Los Angeles Park": "Park Order—Go Away From Grass Today." Into the brilliant lights and moving shadows of his "Kwong On Co., Los Angeles" shuffle two lugubrious, gas-masked figures who give their creator immense private amusement.

Mr. Kingman and his friend Vice-consul Leang and I had lunch. "What we cannot understand is this," said Kingman and Leang, "America got slapped in the face by Japan. Instead of slapping back she turns her back to fight another enemy." They shook their heads and looked amazed. I outlined the familiar arguments for our global strategy, which seemed to me logical. They listened politely. The Chinese always listen politely and with a genuinely interested air. I think they are intrigued by their young, bumptious ally and in many ways impressed. They were not convinced. What all Chinese and their friends wanted was succor for China. But the time when we might have helped her passed when Burma fell. All the sympathy of Americans for China and her cause had not solved the problem of how to reopen the supply route to China without first waging a major campaign in Burma which lies at the outermost extremity of the United Nations' lines.

Bill Shrout, the photographer, and I explored the town. Bill was on his way to the South Pacific to take pictures for *Life*. We wandered around the Presidio, self-consciously returning the salutes of Army men who took us for officers. We hiked over Golden Gate Bridge. We scoured Market Street for more

9

supplies. Since Bill intended to stay for a year, possibly the duration—where I was only going for a few months—his list of needs was immeasurably longer; in fact, had no end. From San Francisco all the way across the Pacific Bill haunted shops ashore, ships' small stores, Army Post Exchanges and quartermaster depots on a tireless hunt for clothing, medicines, toilet articles, notions. Besides his personal gear he had to lug around five cameras and three foot-lockers filled with photographic material. I never saw any photographer who went through more travail in his work.

Charlie Murphy was also in San Francisco. Charlie is a large, handsome man with greying temples and the graceful, commanding air of a full-rigged clipper ship. He is a veteran journalist who in 1934 went to the South Pole with Admiral Byrd to report the Antarctic expedition. A more recent chapter in Charlie's glamorous career was the sinking of the freighter *Zamzam* on which he was en route to Africa a few months before the United States entered the war. Charlie with the rest of the *Zamzam's* survivors was taken aboard the German raider which made the attack. He not only assumed command of the survivors but very nearly assumed command of the raider too, judging by reports that came back.

Charlie was an old, friendly antagonist of mine. He had gone out of his way to belabor the Maritime Commission for discouraging, he charged, a wonderful scheme for beating the U-boat campaign. The scheme was the *Sea Otter,* a design for a small, shallow-draft cargo ship propelled by a series of Chrysler engines mounted on vertical propeller shafts. Charlie's indignant thesis was that Washington bureaucracy had torpedoed the *Sea Otter* before it had a fair trial. I had gone out of my way to attack the *Sea Otter.* My thesis was that it had had a fair trial, that it had proven to be impractical, and that the only reason the idea had stayed alive as long as it had was because Colonel Knox and the President had got themselves out on a limb with a premature endorsement of it. After the tests they had hesitated to give the *Sea Otter* the quick death it deserved. "Little Stinker" was the title of the story I wrote.

Since Charlie's and my stories appeared almost simultaneously—his in *Fortune,* mine in *Time*—there was some con-

10

fusion around the company and Charlie and I were invited to argue our cases before a one-man tribunal, as it were. The meeting adjourned with each of us convinced he was still right and the one-man tribunal still perplexed.

We got together and re-argued the case, discussed strategy and the postwar world, had our pictures taken together in a San Francisco nightclub and ended up behaving like a pair of Elks. Charlie's envy of my assignment was exhilarating.

But I was beginning to wonder if my assignment would ever come off. I began to look on San Francisco with impatience. The city was aware of the war the way the rest of the country was aware of it. Among the citizens there was an air of adventure, in some cases a feeling of compulsion. But there was little comprehension. In only a few cases was there a sense of tragedy and that was personal and not shared. It was the Administration's policy then to minimize that aspect. There were to be no stories about the dead and maimed. The country was irritated but not badly hurt. There was no passionate resolution about the war. The nation had no idea what was happening over the rim. And when I thought about it, neither had I.

One day, finally, my orders came. I was to report at a certain transport dock before three o'clock on the following afternoon. I was to make my departure with great secrecy and on no account was I to send any wires revealing these plans. I wrote a letter to Peg, who had been writing faithfully to me. They had been getting the winter cover off the tulips. It had rained and rained. They had been to see *In Which We Serve,* which the girls thought was "swell." Nancy had a new blue suit for Easter. Peg had gone into New York to get the twins new dresses. "I finally found two just the same. The dresses are navy blue faille with white collars—very plain and demure but very becoming and they fit perfectly. I got the 4:55 home and as I plodded up our street with these prizes I could see two grimy gals in slacks, pants rolled up, plaid shirts, muddy shoes, with filthy hands and faces, playing marbles—but they were very thrilled with the fancy clothes. . . . We miss you so much but wish you a good trip and safe return."

I washed out some undershirts and shorts because I knew the hotel laundry would never get them back to me in time. After

11

all the waiting I felt the sudden crowding of time. I draped my dubious-looking wash over the shower curtain rail, went to bed and slept restlessly. The next day I checked out and on a bright afternoon taxied madly across San Francisco to the pier. This was the real beginning. There was a warlike atmosphere around the docks, fenced in as they were, patrolled by armed guards. Bill was already on the dock and had got his gear aboard. His precious foot-lockers had had to go in the hold. He escorted me to the Officer of the Deck who stood at the top of the gangway. Bill, who had been with the Atlantic Fleet and was a great stickler for regulations anyway, cautioned me to face aft and salute the flag as I stepped aboard. Then I must salute the O.D. I performed these rites raggedly but with a nonchalant air, feeling as though I were stepping off the end of the world.

A man can prepare himself for almost anything but an anticlimax. I had expected that we would steal from San Francisco that night and that morning would find us at sea crawling through the fog and disappearing over the horizon. But instead, so the O.D. informed me as he returned my salute, we were not to sail that night, he could not say when we would sail, we could spend the evening ashore so long as we were back aboard by seven the next morning. Excitement went flatter than a fallen cake. Bill showed me our tiny cabin, where I stowed my gear, and we walked down the gangplank wondering what in the world to do.

We mooned around Fisherman's Wharf and climbed the tower on Telegraph Hill. We ate a silent, anticlimactic supper and went to a movie show. Around eleven we wandered back to the ship. We discovered that we had another cabinmate—Ira Wolfert of North American Newspaper Alliance, who had already laid himself out on the only lower berth. We woke him up to introduce ourselves, crawled up onto our shelves under a labyrinth of mysterious pipes and, still landbound, slept.

In the morning we were still tied to the dock. Our ship, a transport, was crowded with troops. We stood around speculating on how long it would be before we pulled out. One opinion was that we would stay here several days at least. But around eleven o'clock, with bombers roaring overhead making practice passes at us, in full view of San Francisco's crowded

12

waterfront, we steamed down the bay and under the Golden Gate Bridge. Aboard our ship were six women and some 2200 men. We were on our way through the 2090 miles of sea which stretched between us and Pearl Harbor.

II

PARADE IN OVERALLS

I<small>T WAS NOT LITERALLY TRUE</small> that America had turned her back on the Pacific. In spite of the demands of the Mediterranean theatre in the spring of 1943 we were steadily moving quantities of sea-borne and air-borne supplies across five to seven thousand miles of Pacific Ocean. We were sending into the sunsets over the rim of the world millions of tons of shipping—landing ships, warships, transports, tankers, merchantmen—loaded with Spam, beef, beer, canned vegetables, canned fruits, atabrine, quinine, salt pills, condoms, shoes, socks, shirts, blankets, pontoons, cranes, oil, jeeps, trucks, tanks, bulldozers, rifles, grenades, howitzers, ammunition, and thousands of bored, angry, wise-cracking American soldiers.

We had already gathered enough strength to get up off our knees after the stunning knock-down of December 7, and though I did not know—but suspected—we were preparing that April for the first blows of a new offensive.

Aboard our transport we settled down to an eight- or nine-day voyage that was gay and glamorous in peacetime but was neither of those things now with the strictures of wartime.

Evenings before sunset a bosun piped a warning warble into the ship's public address system and announced: "The smoking lamp is out on all weather decks," and after that there was no smoking or lighting of matches out on deck and for anyone caught at it by the watchful patrols swift punishment followed, whatever the rank of the culprit.

Sitting on the blacked-out decks got to be a bore. The lighted wardroom was sweltering. Our cabin was overcrowded with three. We had to edge crabwise around each other to get at the sink to shave, to dress and to get out the door. We had no

14

complaint. These quarters were luxurious compared to the troops'.

Some of the troops slept on the weather decks in hammocks and canvas cots where the air was good but likely to be wet. The others slept on pipe berths in the crowded holds and 'tween decks where the air was foul even with the blowers going. The air was bad enough in our cabin with all portholes closed on account of the blackout. Daytime the troops packed the decks, where there was scarcely more than standing room. They were mostly men of a Navy Construction Battalion. There were also a number of Negro civilian workers aboard on their way to jobs in Honolulu. They wore an anxious, watchful expression and managed to keep apart.

In our officers' quarters on the deck above we were able to play shuffleboard, lie in deck chairs, promenade. In the wardroom we stuffed ourselves on dinners of fruit cup, soup, filet mignon, potatoes, frozen peas, salad, hot rolls, celery, olives, milk, coffee, tea, strawberry parfait, cheese and crackers. The only limit was a man's appetite. I recall an ensign consolidating a breakfast of wheat cakes which he had ordered and a plate of eggs and bacon which had appeared by mistake—draping the eggs over the cakes and quickly disposing of the whole business. The Seabees took what was doled out to them as they filed past the soup kettles and ate their beans and stew off their laps. I saw no evidence of anyone going hungry, but I preferred the officers' mess.

Even the stars at night looked hot, shining on the fringes of the clouds and glowing in the sea. We lay on top of our berths perspiring with the fan whirring and the blower roaring. The enlisted men spent hours below waiting in line at the soda fountain. The mechanical cow, fed powdered milk, water, and butter, gushed forth milk and cream from her metal teat for ice cream. Mr. Young, the executive officer, took me on a tour of the ship. We climbed down iron ladders. Gratings treacherous with a film of oil led around our ship's massive laboring machinery. Over all was the oppressiveness of heat, confinement and noise, and the stench of hot oil. We went into the boiler room through an airlock, dogging down the iron doors behind us. A sudden rush of air would have caused a back draft and

15

the men in the boiler room would have been seared by the belch of flames. The glow from the boiler's white-hot eyes glinted on the brass instrument cases and on naked, wet backs. The men were amazingly nonchalant working in their hell-hole.

We went aft into the crew's dark, crowded quarters. In a ten-celled brig sat a disconsolate man in an undershirt; his crime was insolence. We went into the sick bay. Half a dozen men in hospital shirts lay on double-deck berths. There was the hospital odor of disinfectant and ether. In a small operating room the doctors were getting ready to perform an appendectomy and a signalman lay doubled up on the table while an attendant held him by the head and knees and the surgeon took a sight on his spine, preparatory to injecting the anesthesia. Above his white face-mask the surgeon's black eyes were intent. He cut through the fat. I was reminded of slitting the fat bellies of croakers on fishing trips on the Eastern Shore. Neatly he cut, laboriously he sorted out the signalman's insides, fastening and refastening clamps, perspiring in the heat of the glaring overhead lights, until at last he came up with it—a straggly-looking appendix which he held on high in his gloved fingers like a trophy.

Two days out, four days out, six days out of San Francisco. The appendectomy patient felt better. A major in the Medical Corps absent-mindedly wandered out on deck smoking an after-dinner cigar and was confined to his quarters for the rest of the voyage. The major, who was a dentist, was a luckless man anyhow. I heard afterward that when he reported in at the airfield in Honolulu where he was to be attached, he discovered that someone had made a mistake in his papers and had classified him as a mechanic. There was a flurry of excitement. We were at the second mess in the evening when General Quarters sounded and we rushed to our stations. Several hundred yards away, across the rolling grey sea, another transport plowed along abreast of us. The destroyer escort was out of sight. There was not much talking, only an uneasy waiting. Several of the women began to laugh nervously. We were very acutely aware of our helplessness.

It was a false alarm. Two ships, sighted hull down on our port beam, had failed to identify themselves promptly. One destroyer finally returned to her patrol, zigzagging back and forth ahead of our own zigzagging course. We waddled on across the Pacific with the sea rolling out from under our stern.

The Seabees' band played jive and martial airs on the quarterdeck. It was the only band I heard in the whole Pacific until I got to Australia and heard a boys' school band pumping out "God Save the King" one Sunday afternoon in a park. The Pacific war is a dungaree war. Evenings in the smoke-filled wardroom we listened to the electric organ played by a member of the ship's crew who had once been organist in a San Francisco movie house. The Seabees entertained us. They were talented men, these carpenters and plumbers, who could play pianos, guitars, accordions, violins. The officers liked hillbilly tunes and things like "You'd Be So Nice to Come Home to."

We correspondents discussed our jobs and our accomplishments. We were a small-sized journalistic convention. Also aboard was Rembert James, of Associated Press, a quiet, apologetic man who went out and got his toes mashed and an eardrum ruptured by a shrapnel blast. During his sojourn in the Pacific Jim interviewed a head-hunter in the Solomons. I could imagine Jim gulping: "Pardon me, chief, but you say that after you get these heads . . ."

We all deferred to Ira then. Ira had been in Guadalcanal and therefore commanded everyone's attention. Ira was the most unwarlike looking of all war correspondents, with a face like a full moon and a great, broad behind, and a knack of wearing Army khakis so that they looked like a sports outfit which he had donned for a day at the beach. Bill, Jim, and I tried to look more martial.

Lena was a nurse. She had been in Pearl Harbor on December 7. Most of her patients had been burn victims, she related, and she had some recollections of horror which she would never forget and now and then described. Lena had gone back to the States and now was returning to a Honolulu hospital. She was a big, blonde girl with a hearty manner. There was another nurse, a Pole from New York, awed by her adventure. She had had a good job. "But I wanted to do somet'ing in the war." She curled up in a deck chair like a little brooding hen eyeing the world over her bosom. There was a sphynxlike wife of a Marine captain who remarked occasionally that she thought Ira was a riot but otherwise remained aloof. The other females on our crowded transport were three ladies on their way to office jobs in Honolulu who made the most of their novel situation.

Lieutenant Commander Walter Blue, boss of the Seabees, was a gaunt, towering man with a clipped black moustache. I later met a major in Guadalcanal who knew him. "Sure—Little Boy Blue!" Blue had lived in St. Louis, where he had been a construction engineer. He had worked on the Detroit-Windsor tunnel. He was in his fifties, I judged. He had been a private in the last war and I asked him how he happened to get into this one.

"I figured no job—nobody's job would be any good until we licked the little bastards," he said. "I had already raised a family and I told my wife I was going to join. She thought they would never take me because I'm color blind. Anyhow she said, 'Go ahead,' and they took me. They were glad to get me."

He was proud of his men. Most of them were past their twenties—artisans, plumbers, machinists, carpenters, who could have been making high wages back home and could have got into defense jobs and been deferred. They were men, Blue said, who reasoned pretty much the way he had.

If that was true then their ideas were more concrete than those of most of the young officers—newly hatched ensigns from college training centers, Air Corps men, Service Force men, medical men. I asked a Service Force lieutenant what he was fighting for. "Oh, hell—Uncle Sam," he said. I asked him if he and his colleagues didn't ever discuss war aims and fascism and democracy and so on and he said, no, he never heard any discussions. He was in the war because he didn't have any choice in the matter, frankly. I talked to a Medical Corps man, an intelligent Jewish boy in whom I would have expected to find more passion. "What we talk about is getting home," he said. "All we want is to get it over with."

They took it for granted that life in the United States was going to be just the same when they got back. That was what they hoped, at least. They had no great hatred for the enemy; if they were embarked on a crusade they did not know it. They had no mottoes. They had no ideologies which they could put into words, or which anyone had put into words for them. This was just a lousy business which had to be tended to.

Before a yellow backdrop rigged up on a lower deck Max Beck, the ship's chaplain, conducted church services. The pulpit was a table on which were two white candles and a silver cross. Officers sat, enlisted men stood behind, and we filled to overflowing the well between the midship superstructure and the poop. Behind young Max the snout of a five-inch gun pointed out to sea, where a brown albatross soared lazily alongside.

The tones of the electric organ rose above the sound of our rushing wake. Six solemn Seabees in blues were the choir. We opened our hymnals and sang, "Holy, Holy, Holy! All the saints adore Thee." We also sang, "Faith of Our Fathers—God's great power shall win all nations unto Thee, and through the truth that comes from God mankind shall then be truly free...." And "Have we trials and temptations, is there trouble everywhere? We should never be discouraged. Take it to the Lord in prayer." Max led us in prayer: "Be with us wherever we are sent.... Be with us wherever we are. Be with our President. Bless our loved ones at home.... May peace again come on earth...."

The Seabees' chaplain preached the sermon, his text the parable of the talents. It meant, he said, that we must use our God-given abilities, not bury them away or hide them under a bushel. He was an earnest but not particularly eloquent man. It seemed to me the talents of his congregation were peaceful talents which would have to remain buried for some time. I remembered what Blue said: "I figured nobody's job would be any good until we licked the little bastards."

The chaplain disapproved of what he called foxhole religion, he said. "It is not Christianity to turn to religion merely because you're scared." He also disapproved of fatalism, he said. But the prevailing philosophy of his audience was: "If you're gonna get it you're gonna get it." Said the chaplain: "Men must have faith in God's plan." The audience began to fidget and gaze blankly at the swooping albatross. They felt better standing on their feet and singing: "Jesus calls us o'er the tumult of life's wild, restless sea."

I tried to take a sight on things. We were going down into

19

the valley that spring of 1943, fighting a kind of guerrilla-like intellectual war—swearing, arguing, and praying that we would get back up on the other side. It was a year and four months since the Japs had stung us into a rage. Now the rage had gone, leaving us with cold anger but no consuming idea. There was not even pomp or circumstance to help us forget that we had no clear conception of what we were fighting for. We were a drab parade of machines and men in overalls. We were brave and ingenious and dogged enough to win the Pacific war, but we might not be smart enough to win the peace. The best we were able to do was keep our faith in what we had known in America, even though for a lot of us it had never been too good.

We used to listen to the radio in Young's cabin. One night we tuned in Tokyo and heard the ingratiating voice of a woman speaking in English and describing the plausible aims of Japan to bring peace and prosperity to Asia. We switched to New York and picked up a hubbub of Town Hall of the Air. There were many voices but the one which blared out above all others was Senator Styles Bridges' denouncing government by directives, government spending that was leading to bankruptcy. In the middle of the blacked-out Pacific all the faraway voices seemed unreal and unrelated. Our small, rolling ship-world was the only reality. And in the midst of the worries and prejudices and preaching and confused thinking aboard there was nevertheless one great singleness of purpose: to get ourselves safely across 2090 miles of sea. Day after day we guarded against showing any lights after blackout, refrained from throwing cigarette butts or refuse into the ocean where they might leave a wake and betray us to the enemy, and lined up obediently for General Quarters—while the captain studied his charts and ruminated in his cabin, and men stood ceaseless watch and the pistons pumped and the ship rocked along on her zigzag course and pale people leaned over the rail being seasick and anxious.

We raised the Hawaiian Islands late in the morning of the following day. Oahu materialized on our starboard bow; Koko Head; the mountains with their blue shoulders in a cloud, Oahu's dark and cottony mantle which hangs there perpetually spilling "liquid sunshine" onto the hills and sometimes into the valleys. All of the volcanic islands in the Pacific have their private cover of clouds. Even on a clear day when there is not another cloud in the whole sky, a voluptuous mass will be snagged on a spiny little island in the middle of the otherwise empty sea.

We rounded Diamond Head into Honolulu Harbor, steamed toward the plain of Hickam Field and Pearl Harbor beyond, threaded our way in between the Naval Station and the bright green flats around the Pan-Am airdrome. Shore installations, docks, cranes had a strangely theatrical look in the hot, bright sunshine. There were incongruous looking palm trees. We crawled past the rusted, partly exhumed battleship *Oklahoma*, past an American flag flapping over the bonepile of the *Arizona*, past businesslike looking warships at their moorings and with our Seabee band tooting edged into our berth.

Motor scooters, bicycles, station wagons, trucks and lorries rolled in and out of long warehouses. Men in dungarees stood on the long pier gazing at us with no particular welcome. We gazed back. A sunburned man draped over the fender of a parked truck looked up at our crowded rails. "Hello, suckers," he suddenly bellowed. The men on the decks below shouted back at him but I couldn't make out what they said. The man beside the truck blew a Bronx cheer. "Aw, wait until you've been here a while. Wait until you've seen some action, wise guys."

We were not to be allowed to disembark until morning although the unloading of cargo began immediately. Cargo hatches were lifted, booms began to swing and there was the loud rattle and screech of wire cables running through blocks. When night abruptly closed down the stevedores went on working under floodlights. The night was quiet, except for the racket of the unloading.

The next morning we disembarked. I watched the Seabees, dressed in green overalls, file down the gangplank lugging packs, bedding, steel helmets, rifles. They lined up in ragged, encumbered files. There they stood for a long time, looking restlessly to their officers for the next order. A column of trucks finally rolled out on the dock and all the men and their gear were

21

bundled in and carted off. That was the last I saw of Little Boy Blue's Construction Battalion.

I saw the little Polish nurse from New York State standing in the shade of a warehouse waiting for someone. She looked frightened, forgotten and forlorn.

III

HONOLULU

THERE WAS MAIL FOR ME in Honolulu. Joan, one of the twins, had pecked out a letter on a typewriter. They had spent a week-end at my sister's cottage at Lake Estling. Joan wrote: "We came home yesterday after a very delightful and swell vacation. Friday morning we got up early and went fishing. I caught one shiner but it was too small so I threw it back in. We spent most of our time down at the lake on the beach, playing Red Rover, Red Light and Giant Strides until we were bored with them. Once when I was being chased I started to jump over the railing but I missed. Thank goodness there was nice soft sand at the bottom. I fell right on my chin and cut my lips but was relieved to find my teeth and braces had not been damaged. I am fully recovered now however...."

Joan also brought me up to date on some of the events of the past couple of weeks: "Easter Sunday as usual all choirs sang both services. In between the children's choir got ice cream. The first service was quite full and quite warm but the second was the limit. It was filled to the brim and stifling. By the time Dr. Butz had finished his sermon which was forceful as it was he was as red as a beet and dripping from head to foot. We were too.... We all miss you very much and all send love. Hurry home. Your loving daughter...."

I had a small pang of homesickness.

Bill and I got a room at the Halekulani Hotel. It had a screened-in *lanai* and looked out through the palms onto Waikiki Beach and Diamond Head. Our firm's Honolulu man, Bernie Clayton, was in the States but he had considerately left the firm's ponderous Oldsmobile at our disposal. Being a newsman, and a citizen, I was anxious to inspect the country's chief

Pacific outpost. This more or less fitted into Bill's plans for visiting all the quartermasters' depots and Post Exchanges on the island of Oahu, so that in the course of sight-seeing we also acquired steel helmets, gas masks, first aid kits, canteens, camera supplies, shoes and odds and ends.

Oahu was pass-crazy. Every public building contained a bureau which issued some kind of pass. For almost every step a man took or action he performed he had to have a pass. At least that was what old Honolulu hands told us and because Bill began to worry that he would find himself in a situation without the proper pass we began to collect passes.

We stood in line by the hour getting fingerprinted and photographed. Before we got through I estimated that in various files and desk drawers in Honolulu were at least forty-three impressions of my fingers. We collected an "Employer's Certificate" permitting us to be on the streets after the ten o'clock curfew; a "Personal Identification" certifying that we were a resident of Honolulu; a license as an "Auto Gas Operator," nonrenewable if the licensee was convicted of "furious, heedless or reckless driving"; and an "Identification Certificate" which stated that we had been duly registered under the Hawaiian Defense Act and which qualified us to apply for a "Purchase Permit," which in turn allowed us to buy one bottle a week of rationed liquor. Bill did not drink but he got a Purchase Permit anyhow after Ira and I persuaded him that he might want to buy a bottle for a friend.

In addition there were certain cards issued by the military authorities: accreditation as a Press Correspondent to the U.S. Pacific Fleet; a pass to the Navy Yard; and a "Certificate of Assimilation" bearing a two-inch-square photograph, prints of the right hand and the statement that "Duncan Norton-Taylor (Reporter) is assimilated to the Army of United States with rank of 2nd Lieutenant and in accordance with the provisions of the Geneva Convention of July 27, 1929 (G.W.P. title VII Article 81) is entitled to be treated as a prisoner of war in the event he falls into the hands of the enemy and is detained." This meant that I could claim the pay of a Second Lieutenant if I fell into the hands of the enemy. I used to take this card out of my bulging wallet and study it for long, uneasy moments.

24

Oahu under martial law was not the place that prewar travel folders described. I suspected that in some respects it never had been that place. Waikiki Beach turned out to be so narrow that most of it was under water at high tide. Although the famous breakers creaming across the ocean were superb for surfing, bathers were occasionally discouraged by the remnants of a *luau* (Hawaiian feast). One bather, a Marine, was taken aback when he swam headfirst into the entrails of a pig. He thought it was a pig.

Honolulu began folding itself up for the night along about late afternoon. Some stores closed as early as 3:30 because of the shortage of help and the lack of merchandise. By eight o'clock the blackout was complete and frightening. Streets were deserted except for knots of people hurrying home from the last movie show. Cars and busses crept cautiously along the highways. Regulation hoods over their headlights cut illumination down to practically nothing and dim overhead lights—a relaxation of the original stringent rules put in force after December 7, 1941—made driving only slightly less hazardous. By ten o'clock the whole island was as dark and still as death.

In the Territory of Hawaii, most vital point in America's western defenses, lived some 157,000 people of Japanese birth—37 per cent of the Territory's population; 121,000 of them were American citizens; 36,000 of them were still aliens—enemy aliens since December 7, 1941.

This was one reason for the ten o'clock curfew. Lieutenant General Delos Emmons, since succeeded by Lieutenant General Robert Richardson, Jr., wanted to keep them off the streets at night so that, as Bob Trumbull of the *New York Times* said, the Army would at least know where they ought to be after ten o'clock. The Army also wanted to keep the streets clear for any emergency movement of troops.

It would have been impossible, I was told, to have evacuated all the Japanese in Hawaii or to have clapped all the enemy aliens among them into concentration camps. Besides, many injustices would have resulted from such a drastic program and the economy of Hawaii would have been wrecked. Cheap Japanese labor is the keystone of the Territory's only big industries: sugar, representing an investment of $175,000,000; and pineapples, which were a $54,250,000 export in 1941. If the cheap, efficient, and well-behaved Japs who tend these crops had been withdrawn, Hawaii's banks, newspapers, public services, steamship lines, and the fortunes of the "Big Five" would have probably collapsed.

The Big Five (Alexander & Baldwin, Ltd., American Factors, Ltd., C. Brewer & Co., Castle & Cooke, Ltd., and Theodore H. Davies & Co.) ruled Hawaii's roost. They are the descendants of the Yankee missionaries who first colonized the islands, and they own or control all of Hawaii's banks, newspapers, public services, steamship lines, and sugar and pineapple plantations. They imported the Japanese in the first place and have always felt solicitous about them. In prewar days plantation owners even contributed to Shinto shrines. Shintoism is Emperor worship which before December 7 seemed harmless enough, even quaint. When the Emperor's planes appeared over Oahu the Big Five were as frightened as everybody else, until it appeared that the danger had passed. Then they spread their wings over their chicks and even cackled indignantly when such cheap, well-behaved labor was referred to impolitely as "Jap." The military authorities interned some 1400 Shinto worshipers suspected of subversive activities. The loyalty of the other Japanese will probably never be put to the test since Hawaii now is in no danger of invasion.

The Army took us on a tour of its installations one day and showed us beaches festooned with barbed wire, coast artillery emplacements, hidden ack-ack nests, mile after mile of landing fields, revetments, hangars, maintenance shops. Oahu's 387,000 acres and 149 miles of coastline are now armed to the teeth. Details were censored, but it was apparent that if the Japs attacked today the story would be different. The story of the war would have been different if Hawaii had been as well prepared before December 7, 1941.

The development of Hawaii as a virtually impregnable fortress, however, has raised a new spectre for the Big Five. Hawaii's present-day military strength has been built by thousands of workers sent by the government from the States. America has invested millions of dollars in roads, hospitals, military installations. About half of the labor, according to a nervous estimate in *Thrum's Hawaiian and Standard Guide,* is employed by private construction companies. Many of them—skilled and unskilled—are union men. They like the climate and many of them intend to stay. The old owners and managers of Hawaii's feudalism regard the future with misgivings and get what inspiration they can from reading Westbrook Pegler in the *Honolulu Advertiser* as they gulp their Kona coffee in the sunny morning.

In the sunny morning big gray busses jammed with workers rolled along Kalakaua Avenue toward the city. Automobiles, for which Hawaiians paid fantastic prices, filled Honolulu's streets. Honolulu stands about midway between Waikiki and Pearl Harbor, which lie at either end of a fifteen-mile-long coastal flat. All across the hot and steamy flat overburdened highways crawled with traffic. The ridiculous little Oahu Railway trains huffed-puffed around the shores of Honolulu Harbor with workers hanging out of the windows and spilling onto the platforms of the wooden cars. Long convoys of military trucks roared past natives jiggling along in 1936 Fords. The air reeked with gasoline fumes and the heavy sweet perfume of the Dole Pineapple works.

Pretty, scrubbed Honolulu (which is about the size of Jacksonville) was a hodgepodge of East and West. Narrow arteries lined with Oriental shops spilled into broader streets where stood the Big Five's colonnaded commercial buildings, trust companies and modern department store. Behind the city's eight-to-ten-story modern buildings bulged the mountains with their heads in the perpetual clouds. Sometimes the clouds dribbled liquid sunshine into the city's streets, though no one paid much heed to a sprinkling. It took a deluge to ruffle Honolulu. Pink-faced men in Palm Beach suits walked at a deliberate gait so as not to become overheated. The blank-faced Japanese, mixtures of Korean, Chinese, Philippine, Hawaiian, pattered along politely so as not to jostle anyone. In the ethnological potpourri of Hawaii were also the left-overs of Puerto Rican, even English, Irish, German, Yankee. Some of the little black-haired people were fastidiously and fashionably dressed in American clothes. Sloe-eyed girls in the stores and little shops were occasionally beautiful. Their elders, men in coolie hats, women in

27

Mother Hubbards, scuffed along the sidewalks in slapping sandals.

The boys dropped by the accident of war into this onetime glamorous Pacific resort—soldiers, Marines, American sailors in whites, red-bearded British sailors in little boys' shorts—wandered aimlessly around the city. They shopped for souvenirs, gawked at Iolani Palace and Kamehameha I's statue, clustered on street corners or stood in lines to buy a glass of beer. Along River Street the natives gazed indifferently at the sailors lined up on stairways and sidewalks waiting to get into the second-floor bordellos. The houses were only open during the day on account of the curfew and blackout. Around the corner was the prophylactic station and another line-up.

The enlisted man has to stand in line for everything he gets. In a PX a corporal, through a mouthful of peanut candy, poured out his complaint. "We gotta stand in line even for a peanut bar." The corporal had come across the Pacific in a transport that was so crowded they could only serve two meals a day. "By the time you had stood in line and got your first meal and ate it, it was time to go around and get in the chow line again. When I get back to New York," the corporal vowed, "if I even see two guys waiting to buy tickets for a movie I'll say *'Nuts!'* and walk away."

We went with Police Lieutenant Leon Straus on a routine night patrol of Oahu's streets. Everyone at headquarters expected a more or less riotous time because a consignment of mainland liquor had just arrived after a long drought when the only thing to drink, except in the hotels and clubs, was beer and local gin. It looked as though the night would come up to expectations when we drew up almost immediately beside a parked bus and a small crowd of people and found a burly Hawaiian lolling against a tree, bleeding to death. He had been a passenger in the bus. A runt-sized Negro had opened his head with a whiskey bottle. The Negro, standing uncertainly on one foot after the other, was very apologetic. His story was that the Hawaiian had tried to pull him out of his seat and had called him a nigger, so he had broken the whiskey bottle over the gentleman's head. He said he was a cook on a cargo ship. No one seemed to be paying much attention to either of the

28

principals. The crowd, most of whom had been fellow passengers on the bus, were all too busy discussing what each had seen and heard of the fracas. Straus took the Negro into custody and bundled him off in another patrol car. When an ambulance clanged up after what seemed an interminable wait, he got the Hawaiian into it. The Hawaiian struggled and shrieked, evidently in a delirium induced by whiskey and the blow on the head.

We rolled on. As it turned out that was the only excitement. There were six stabbings here and there around the county, which we heard about over Straus's two-way radio, but considering the potentialities I thought this very good and a commentary on the respect which the population had for its cops. Straus was disappointed because he wanted to show us some action.

He emphasized, however, that the Honolulu police force under Chief Gabrielson made a point of being courteous and considerate. The rule was to be especially tolerant of soldiers and sailors.

We stopped by at headquarters and heard the report that the Hawaiian had been badly cut up by the broken bottle but that he would live. The Negro was at headquarters still delivering an elaborate if slightly confused defense of himself. I was impressed by the manner of the Honolulu officers, who were a contrast to many American city cops I had run into in my police reporting days. Gabrielson's men behaved intelligently and like men charged with serving the public. Attached to the force was a volunteer wartime reserve of some 250 businessmen who were always on call for an emergency, actually did one patrol a week, and had the same duties and authorities as the paid regulars.

I asked Straus, whose nickname was "Sonny," what the department's greatest problem was in wartime Honolulu, expecting that it would be the big alien Japanese population, but he said it was juvenile delinquency. With parents in war work, the children were running around wild and getting into various minor and some major scrapes. Boys were committing burglaries. Adolescent girls were getting mixed up with men.

I asked him what section gave him the most trouble by and large and he said, surprisingly, the Waikiki section, which includes the swank hotels and the pretty, palm-bordered neigh-

29

borhoods around them. Sonny said he was always getting complaints and having to rush out to the Waikiki section. "You go into a respectable-looking bungalow where the trouble is and the first thing you see is some tart who used to work the streets down in Honolulu. Now she is the lady of the house." A lot of Honolulu girls, he explained, had taken advantage of the war to "shack up" with lonesome and well-heeled civilian workers from the States and had assumed a new dignity in the community. But the dignity was pretty thin, Sonny said. The tarts were always getting crocked and raising hell. Waikiki had changed a lot.

IV

CALAMITY HARBOR

CHESTER WILLIAM NIMITZ is a sunburned, apple-cheeked man with cotton-white hair and sky-blue eyes who looks more like a Texas farmer than a four-star admiral. In Fredericksburg, Texas, he was born of German stock. The Nimitzes were hotel-keepers. "Cotton-head" Nimitz drove a meat delivery cart and earned a reputation at school as a "rassler." He is a battleship and submarine man, which bothers air enthusiasts, but he is warmly regarded in the Navy, particularly by officers who have served under him. He has a look of stern preoccupation but he is rated as a kindly man, able to handle men, and in no sense a martinet, which a lot of other, older admirals are. Admiral Nimitz is fifty-eight, which is young.

I met the Admiral out at Pearl Harbor. One morning we drove through the colony of pretty bungalows overlooking the harbor, occupied by the Admiral and his staff, drove past the well-kept tennis courts and trim green lawns, and in the long two-story concrete building which houses Cincpac (Commander in Chief of the Pacific Fleet) interviewed the man who was running the Pacific show. The Admiral was in shirt sleeves; the four stars on his collar were the only mark that set him apart from the rest of his khaki-clad officers. In his small, shipshape office he gravely shook hands with each of us, one by one. There were about a dozen correspondents.

What Admiral Nimitz had for the press was advice. He recommended that we study the theories of naval warfare, particularly in the Pacific. It was going to be a long war, and the press should be aware of all the problems. The press should not rush off half-cocked with bad surmises and impossible expectations.

It was clear that the Navy, which had been waiting for the war for almost a quarter of a century, was not to be hurried into any ill-conceived action. The problems must be carefully thought out. Admiral Nimitz was not a man of rash impulses.

I was familiar by this time with the Navy's strategy for the Pacific war, from other conversations and interviews with men on Admiral Nimitz's staff. It was "problematic" whether we could destroy Japan by bombing her homeland. The Navy's use of problematic meant very damn unlikely. The Navy's theory was Clausewitz's: to defeat the enemy you have to destroy his armed forces.

The Navy's ultimate aim was to occupy certain adjacent areas to Japan where it could operate to constrict Japan's economy while striking at her wide-flung armed forces. What areas would these be? We were advised to look at a map and guess, the Navy was not giving such information to the enemy.

The difficulties of the Navy's problems were obvious. Military experience had shown, for instance, that three times as many troops had to be used in attacking an island as the enemy had defending it. Any great Pacific drive must wait until U.S. troops were in far greater strength. Because of the amphibious nature of the problem an all-out offensive depended also on ships. We did not have enough cargo ships and transports in the Pacific in the spring of 1943. Most of the maritime resources of the United States were being concentrated in the Atlantic then. Meanwhile the Navy was fighting a war of annoyance and attrition hitting when and where it could at the perimeter of Jap defenses, which extended then from the Aleutians south through the Marshalls and Gilberts and south to the Solomons.

We were at that moment engaged in attacking Attu. We had been able to concentrate sufficient force against that northern base, which the Japs had snatched during the Battle of Midway, and in the careful mathematics of the Navy the operation should be a success, although Pearl Harbor was waiting news with some suspense because of the imponderable factor always present. The "Jesus factor," one officer called it.

That morning was the only time I saw Admiral Nimitz, except for occasional glimpses of him when he emerged from his office to practice pistol shooting on his special fifty-foot range under the Public Relations office. A stiff, starched Marine patrolled up and down on the road beyond. Another set up a table and on it arranged cartridges and the Admiral's shooting iron. The Admiral blazed away while an aide stood behind him conning the target through a pair of binoculars and calling the shots.

The Navy, like the Army, had come a long way since December 7, 1941. The Admiral could look out his window and see evidences of our new strength below him in the harbor, could read his operational reports and know the strength that was reaching out all over the Pacific. It was seventeen months since the day the enemy had destroyed or disabled eight of the seventeen battleships in our Navy in one short, devastating stroke.

Honolulu people still talked a good deal about that "date that will live in infamy." They will go on talking about it for a long while, which is a good thing, because one day someone will get up and suggest that it is now time to forgive the Japanese people.

Blame for the worst naval defeat in our history has been officially planted on Rear Admiral Husband E. Kimmel and Major General Walter C. Short. They were proud and aloof from one another. They were preoccupied with the old Army-Navy feud, which continued to inhibit operations long afterwards. They were guilty of "dereliction of duty." Yet many others in authority were guilty of the same kind of errors in judgment. Blame for the disaster goes beyond Kimmel and Short and ultimately falls upon all of us. The best informed were flabbergasted when the lightning struck and not until afterward, when they had recovered their breaths and had the benefit of hindsight, did anyone say that the Army and Navy should have anticipated the blow.

For almost a year and a half the Navy had been cleaning up the wreckage. One morning Cincpac stated that it was finally willing to talk about those long and laborious salvage operations. To have publicized them sooner, the Navy said, would have given the enemy too many clues as to our strength, or lack of it. The correspondents in Honolulu gathered in the office of Rear Admiral William Furlong to hear his story.

He began by recounting the events of that Sunday morning as he had witnessed them. He told his story dispassionately and with a remarkable absence of profanity.

He was commander of the Pacific Fleet's minecraft at the time and on the morning of December 7 was aboard the minesweeper *Oglala,* his flagship. He was on the bridge waiting for his mess boy to call him to breakfast, when the first Jap plane appeared. I could imagine Furlong, who looks like a modified version of Jim Farley, strolling around the bridge, patting back a yawn and rubbing his freshly shaved chin when the Jap whined down from the Sunday morning sky and almost within pistol range of him plumped a bomb onto the Ford Island airdrome.

Clustered around Ford Island, which is in the middle of the harbor, were the battleships *California, Maryland, Tennessee, Nevada, Arizona, Oklahoma,* and *West Virginia,* and the repair ship *Vestal.* From where Admiral Furlong stood, staring in astonishment, the old *Utah* would be moored on the other side of Ford Island. The *Oglala* herself was tucked against the mainland, separated from battleship row by a narrow stretch of water. Ahead of her was the cruiser *Helena.* Around the harbor were the rest of the warships and fleet auxiliaries and a floating drydock squatting helplessly under the Jap attack.

The story of how some fifty-odd Japanese dive bombers and torpedo bombers swooped down into the harbor and in approximately half an hour crippled the Pacific Fleet has been told many times. In those tumultous few minutes when Oahu's soft blue sky was fouled by belching smoke, shattered by explosions and spattered with ack-ack, nineteen of our vessels were hit. Disabled were the battleships *Pennsylvania, Maryland, Tennessee,* the cruisers *Helena, Honolulu* and *Raleigh.* Pounded and badly hurt were the battleships *West Virginia, California, Nevada,* the seaplane tender *Curtiss,* and the repair ship *Vestal.* The destroyer *Shaw* had her nose blown off. Furlong's *Oglala* and the destroyers *Cassin* and *Downes* were wrecked. The target ship *Utah,* the floating drydock, the battleships *Arizona* and *Oklahoma* were sunk.

More than 3000 officers and men, who a few minutes before had no idea that the United States was at war, were dead.

Her plates sprung, the *Oglala* had rolled over on her side at

34

her dock. Admiral Furlong was able to step ashore, fortunately unscathed. He was put in charge of salvage about a month later, after Admiral William C. Calhoun got operations started. A private contractor, the Pacific Bridge Company of San Francisco, added its facilities and the talents of its executive officer, A. E. ("Jack") Graham to the work. Furlong was proud to announce for publication that morning that of the nineteen vessels hit all but three had left the harbor. The carcasses of the *Cassin* and *Downes* had been broken up for scrap. The three left were the *Arizona, Oklahoma,* and *Utah.* All the others had been patched up and had left Pearl Harbor under their own power—either for active service or to return to the States for further repairs. How many were still immobilized Furlong would not say.

Furlong took us in his launch across the dirty harbor waters to see the last three still resting there, memorials to America's false peace.

We climbed gingerly aboard the *Oklahoma,* which had been righted, and now rested on the harbor's bottom with just her port rail awash. Furlong's salvage superintendent, Commander F. H. Whittaker, explained the prodigious process of righting the 29,000-ton elephant. The Japs' torpedoes, exploding with extraordinary destructiveness, had opened up her port side and the weight of the water pouring in had capsized her before counter-flooding measures could be taken to keep her on an even keel. She had rolled completely over. Stack and masts had snapped off and she had lain there, upside down, her superstructure half buried in the soft grey mud and just her bottom showing above the surface. Through holes cut in her bottom, divers had gone down into the flooded, viscous blackness of the hulk, bumped by the corpses of their former shipmates. Working by feel, they had patched the holes in her sides. Coffer dams were built. Compartments, finally sealed, were pumped out and she was lightened as much as possible by removing anchor chains and all heavy, loose gear.

From winches anchored onto the shore of Ford Island the salvagers ran out steel cables which they made fast to the *Oklahoma*'s bottom. As they hauled away on the cables, rolling the big ship over inch by inch, they emptied more compartments,

35

moved the cables around to new positions on the hull. The process took months. Over the long period of patching, pumping and hauling the winches turned a total of sixty-nine hours, moving the elephant at the rate of two degrees an hour. The process went on until the old ship finally lifted her muck-covered turrets and topsides out of the water and lay there within two degrees of being rightside up.

We walked solemnly along her wooden decks, which were pocked with the borings of marine worms. Whittaker, a tall, long-faced Texan, said that she had been covered with barnacles but most of them had been scraped off. Her topsides were bent and buckled after months of supporting the whole crushing weight of her hull. Bulkheads, turrets, deck gear— everything was slimy and black with oil. From her open hatches drifted the nauseous odor of gas, formed by the rotted remains of vegetables, meats, supplies and 381 men still unaccounted for.

Workmen wearing gas masks climbed stolidly down inside her, crawled out black and foul. I looked at them with a curious sense of shame and revulsion.

Furlong explained that when a skeleton was recovered it was put in a bag and turned over to the medical department. Identification in most cases was impossible. Most of the men had not worn name tags: "dog tags," which now Army and Navy men all wear.

The once elaborate captain's cabin was a soiled ruin. The leather was decaying from the chairs. Some of the captain's watersoaked record forms lay beside a misshapen safe. Linoleum on the deck was buckled and mouldering. Portlights were broken. The cork-lined overhead was caving in but hanging from it was a fragile white light globe freakishly intact. In the dark, blackened compartment that had once been the crew's mess the long bone of a man's arm or leg lay in plain sight in a ray of sunshine that came through an empty doorway. I wondered, shocked, why someone did not remove it. In another corner of the galley was a charred, rubber-heeled shoe.

Whittaker matter-of-factly said that he thought the *Oklahoma*'s old-fashioned reciprocating engines had been pretty well protected by the oil. Admiral Furlong said that she would be floated, reconditioned and would some day steam out of

36

Pearl Harbor under her own power. There was still a lot of cleaning up to do, he added almost apologetically, and took us over to look at the *Arizona*.

The *Arizona*'s bow was out of sight. Some of her after part stuck out gauntly above the water. She had gone down on an even keel but with her belly blown out by a bomb that went down her stack. We stood silently on wooden platforms built above her grave. Past redemption, she was being picked clean and broken apart. Her huge turret mechanisms were being cut away and lifted out to be used elsewhere, probably ashore. Her main and second batteries had all been recovered and so had the ammunition from her after magazines. In her submerged wreckage were the skeletons of 1071 officers and men.

The battered old *Utah* had been occupying the berth of an aircraft carrier that Sunday morning and the Japs had mistaken her identity—one of their few mistakes. She still lay upside down with her broad iron bottom protruding above the harbor, hot and bare beneath the sun. Salvage operations were just getting started. Several holes had been cut in her hull and divers were being lowered inside. The divers, enlisted men specially trained, were paid extra compensation: five dollars an hour or any part of an hour they worked. I would not have done the work for twice that. There was no lightheartedness among them. Even at the nastiest kind of work Americans usually manage a casual, cheerful air. But there was none of that among these men. Some of the divers on the *Oklahoma* and *Arizona* had had to quit, unable to stand the horror of it.

There were still the remains of fifty-seven men inside the *Utah* but after a year and a half under water there would be very little left. I had an uncomfortable feeling walking across that iron coffin.

A rubber-suited diver emerged from one of the holes. He was a grotesque, slime-covered creature out of his element in the sun. He had to be guided to a bench and helped onto it and there he squatted without moving, hands hanging over knees, while two men fell upon him, wrenching and twisting at his monstrous head until they finally lifted it off. The little head of a man underneath looked utterly incongruous. He sat there with face blank, while they pulled off his rubber suit.

37

Now that the harbor was virtually cleaned up, Furlong said, the job was not getting a high priority rating. They worked at it when they could. Any emergency repairs, such as patching a torpedo hole in an aircraft carrier, always got first attention. There were bits and pieces to retrieve and the experts liked to probe the wreckage so that they could estimate the weapons with which the enemy had struck. There were many lessons to be learned. There were indeed, I reflected.

Furlong said there was little more to see. We got back in the launch and chugged across the grey, dirty harbor. We had had a convincing demonstration of the destructiveness of modern war. A year after the event the American people had been shown some pictures of the calamity—pictures of rolling smoke, vomiting fire and twisted wreckage. They were terrifying and dramatic pictures. But the Navy has never shown the most terrifying pictures of all—the burned and twisted wreckage of human bodies. No pictures will ever show the agony of dying men on that sunny Sunday morning.

V

"MAY GOD BE WITH YOU"

I WAS READY TO MOVE ON and had applied for transportation by
air to the South Pacific area. But so had Wolfert and Shrout—
days before I had—and they were still waiting. There was no
way of hurrying things up outside of bullying the Army Transport Command, who were imperturbable. The ATC would
send us south when they had room, which might be any day
now. We should be ready to go at a few hours' notice. Still we
waited.

I had heard of the nostalgia which overcomes old Hawaiian
residents when they are separated from their islands. In sun-
drenched Oahu in the middle of the Pacific I began to feel
nostalgic for the rest of the world. The U.S.A. was a never-
never land to which the *Star-Bulletin* and *Advertiser* devoted
a few offhand, sketchy remarks. Even mail from Peg quit coming. Expecting to move on before this, I had told her to start
sending her letters to the South Pacific.

We had a spell of "kona weather"; the wind blew from the
southwest bringing rain. Oahu wilted wetly. In the two-by-
four bar off the Halekulani's dining room where you were
permitted to drink until six in the evening—then the Japanese
bartender anxiously snatched your glass from you—homesick
men asked each other with feeble humor: "What part of the
old country are you from?" I remember the exalted gleam in
the eye of Bob Verrar when he got orders from his firm to
return to America. Hawaiians call it "the mainland."

The war began to seem more remote than it ever had. Occasionally I was awakened in the middle of the night by a racket
that sounded like carpentry but was anti-aircraft batteries practicing. There was an almost constant woosh of planes overhead.

39

But these activities seemed to bear little relationship to the conflict that was being fought 3500 miles away at the other end of the Pacific.

There even seemed to be a sense of remoteness in official quarters. I remember one afternoon Ira, Bill, and I were tramping around Fort Shafter when a voice from the office of the post command roared: "Can't you read? Can't you see we're trying to grow grass there?" Sure enough, we were walking across a little triangle of sick lawn. The sign—*Keep off*—had been knocked down. The indignant voice gave us a long, loud dressing down, winding up: "Keep on the paths around here." We picked up our feet as though we were walking on eggs and took the path around.

The Navy too had its little paths to follow and was not so busy with the war that it could not find time to lecture transgressors. One morning Bill and I went out to the Officers' Club at Pearl Harbor for lunch with two Marines. We were preparing to sit down when a lieutenant commander hove alongside and said icily: "I don't know about you Army fellows but we wear ties at this club." I didn't have on a tie. Everybody went around Pearl Harbor in shirt sleeves and that morning I had discarded my tie. I identified myself as a war correspondent just to save the Army from the stigma but he said not even tieless war correspondents could be served lunch. I reminded him that Admiral Halsey had banished ties completely from the South Pacific. "I don't care what Admiral Halsey does, Admiral Ghormley's order is neckties." He finally permitted me to hide in one corner of the room while one of the Marines got on his motorcycle and chugged over to his barracks for a necktie.

The kona wind petered out and the prevailing northeast trades blew again, bending the palms around the hotel and shaking down the coconuts. I mused over what an ironic fate it would be for a war correspondent to be felled by a coconut and was careful to keep out from under the palms.

I went to a *luau* which Duke and Leocadia Renter gave for some of the soldiers at Fort DeRussy. A *luau* is chiefly pig and *poi*. Pigs are roasted in a hole in the ground, surrounded by hot rocks, covered with canvas, *ti* leaves and earth. I watched barefoot Hawaiian boys exhume our dinner, furiously digging into the earth, finally flipping up the hot rocks and triumphantly lifting out the pork. I was impressed by the way the boys perspired. *Poi,* beloved by Hawaiians, is a light grey mess made of *taro* roots. It resembles paperhanger's paste in consistency and taste. Like everything at a *luau* it is eaten with the fingers. There were hula dancers, who were pretty and little and lithe. There were hula singers, dressed in curtain material, who were mountainous, exuberant and jolly. Experts told me that the performance was not authentic but the boys from DeRussy enjoyed it and so did I.

I considered that I had run the gamut of Hawaiian dining when Bill and I subsequently had dinner at the C. Montague Cookes'. Mrs. Cooke was the hard-working director of Honolulu's USO. Mr. Cooke, an amateur horticulturist, grew orchids in the bark of his monkey pod trees. The Cookes' beautiful dining room looked out across a valley to the legendary peak which was the home of the Hawaiian gods. We ate with knives and forks in pleasant formality.

I poked into other matters. Having heard that a lot of Army nurses had gone to pieces after the horrors of Pearl Harbor I interviewed Colonel Bradfield Smock, head of Tripler Hospital. Colonel Smock told me that out of seventy-four nurses in his hospital on December 7, he had lost only eight: one from nerves, one from arthritis, six from falling in love and getting married. Since then his nurse's staff had expanded with his expanding plant. To show me how composed and efficient the girls were he surrounded me with six of them at lunch. They were all from the mainland—Lieutenants Spearnak and Baker of McKeesport, Pennsylvania, Lieutenant Pesut of Indianapolis, Lieutenant Klein of Keota, Iowa, Lieutenant Anthony of Many, Louisiana, Lieutenant Babezak of Rochester, Minnesota—and all were very bright and happy. The least composed person at the table was I.

Colonel Smock told me that the Medical Corps, nurses and doctors alike, handled the December 7 emergency as though they had rehearsed for just such a catastrophe. He said that only nine casualties had died after the first forty hours; in other words, most of those who had any chance at all of surviving their injuries had been saved by efficient medical attention. He

41

said the Navy's post-disaster casualties were higher than the Army's because of the prevalence of burn casualties among the sailors.

Colonel Smock was proud of his new, mushrooming plant, as he had a right to be. The colonel, a huge, grey, waggish man, had been in the Army twelve years. He confided that he had bought a house on Diamond Head and was going to settle down there ten years hence, when he would be sixty-four and due for retirement.

Word from the Army Transport Command caught us all by surprise. Bill and I had been out to Fort Shafter having lunch with Major Harry Albright and Captain Hugh Lytel and had come back to the hotel planning to spend the rest of the afternoon on the beach. There was a message for Bill to call the ATC. He did immediately. They told him to be at Hickam Field at ten o'clock that night. Bill flew into a paroxysm of packing, while I stood and gnawed my knuckles. They had said nothing about me. The phone rang again and I rushed to it. ATC wanted to know if I knew where Wolfert was. I gave them half a dozen places to try and sat and sulked. But twenty minutes later ATC called again and this time they wanted me. I was told to be at Hickam Field too. I went into a paroxysm of packing.

The phone kept on ringing. ATC was now looking for Rembert James and Art Cohn, of International News Service. The Halekulani switchboard operator phoned to say she thought she had located Ira at the Waikiki movie theatre. She was having him paged. Ira phoned to say that his name had been flashed on the screen and he had rushed back to the hotel and now was packing. INS's Honolulu man Dick Haller phoned to ask if we knew what had happened to Cohn. Charlie O'Brien and Ed Walsh of the Honolulu bureau of OWI stopped in for a farewell drink. Gilbert Cant of the *New York Post* appeared on the scene. He had just arrived from New York and was wistfully soliciting advice. How soon could he get transportation to the South Pacific? We thought Cant really needed very little advice. He had already acquired a jeep and accommodations at the officers' quarters on Ford Island, something none of us had been able to manage. There were ends to tie up, checks to cash, bills to pay. The phone kept ringing and ringing. In a little more than twenty-four hours we should be in the war. Our destination was Noumea in New Caledonia. Cant drank to our happy landing.

It was a dirty night, spitting one of Oahu's sudden rains. Bill and I loaded our gear into the Oldsmobile, stumbling over shrimp plants and bumping into coconut trees around the Halekulani's now blacked-out driveway. We crawled down Kalakaua Avenue through night-time Honolulu and out toward Hickam. The rain splashing against the windshield made visibility worse than ever. We had not allowed enough time and Bill, who was driving, pushed along desperately. He kept muttering, "If we miss this flight——!" Bill never uses profanity. We got to the hangar at Hickam a little after ten, to our relief saw Wolfert, James and Cohn standing by, getting baggage weighed and signing papers. We five were the only passengers. There was a small delegation of Honolulu newspaper men to see us off—Haller, and Charles McMurtry and Befeler of Associated Press. Befeler was going to drive our car back to the hotel.

In a bare, dim-lit room at one end of the hangar we had a briefing in the use of rubber rafts. One was on display—a fat, yellow affair about ten feet long and almost as wide. A solemn ATC officer lectured us, showed us how to pull the trigger which released compressed air and inflated the thing, told us how to set up a radio aerial, which was wound on a spool inside the radio. We should use the folding kite that was part of the equipment if the wind was strong enough to carry it aloft. If not we should attach the aerial to a balloon, also included. There was a can containing some kind of chemicals. If the can was held in sea water the stuff would generate hydrogen to blow up the balloon. The can should be handled with the utmost caution because the chemical would eat holes in the raft. After the aerial had been lifted aloft we could start calling for help. The radio could be set to send an automatic SOS or, with a flick of a switch, transmit a longer message if anyone knew Morse code. The radio was about the size of a small hurdy-gurdy and had to be cranked to generate transmitting power. We must be sure to get on the air at a certain hour when all ships everywhere in the world were required by International Law to stand by and listen for distress signals. There were oars, emergency rations, water, fishing tackle, compass, first aid kit. We listened, trying to commit each step to memory. It was a relief to hear that complete instructions were printed on the radio. "I certainly trust that you will have no use for any of it," said the officer in conclusion, gazing wistfully at all the ingenious equipment. "May God be with you."

We filed outside, carrying musette bags, steel helmets, coats, brief cases. Heavier kit bags were being stowed away for us aboard a big C-87, which was already warming up its engines in the wet. We climbed in. A C-87 is a transport version of the B-24. Its big belly was half filled with freight but there was room left for five reclining seats. We sat down nervously. The big ship rolled smoothly across the field. The four motors swelled into a roar. I peered out the window. The lights on the field began to race past in the darkness. I realized suddenly that we were in the air. The Hawaiian Islands were invisible below us, lost already in the vast black void of the rainy night.

I was headed at last for the theatre of war with my heart in my mouth. The cabin grew cold as we gained altitude despite the heating system. One of the crew came aft and got out some blankets for us. We wrapped ourselves in them and huddled down into our seats. It is amazing how much faith human beings have in their fellow men. We had seen only this one member of the crew but to the rest of them we trustingly handed over our lives—and slept. Under the circumstances there was nothing else we could do.

VI

THE RIM

I WOKE AT DAYBREAK. The sun was coming up over a blanket of clouds spread below us, turning into a glowing pink and white field. Clouds frighten the life out of me sometimes. Sitting in the cabin of a plane with nothing to do but morbidly speculate I imagine myself having the urge to step out into those thick, solid-looking banks. Then I begin to have titillations of terror.

Through occasional breaks I could see the blue Pacific, some nine thousand feet below. We suddenly banked. Below us was a flat white atoll. At 8:30 in the morning we circled and sat down lumberingly on the island of Canton, 1900 miles from Hickam Field.

Canton lies shriveling under the sun just a few degrees south of the equator. The inside of our cabin was hot before we landed. We stepped out onto an airfield that was like the top of an oven. The island is nothing more than a horseshoe of white coral sand around a shimmering, warm light green lagoon. Outside of one much-photographed palm tree it is virtually bare of vegetation. Every once in a while in those days the Japs winged over at night, probably from Tarawa in the Gilberts, 950 miles to the west, and dropped a few bombs. Their targets were the American garrison's brown, unpainted shacks, khaki tents, ammunition and fuel dumps, aircraft which were parked between white coral revetments, and anti-aircraft emplacements along Canton's blank shores.

We washed in fresh water distilled from sea water and had a breakfast of eggs at the officers' mess. The mess attendants told us that there was rarely any meat and almost never any fresh vegetables. Between supply ships they sometimes ran low on stores, but so far no one had gone hungry. Beer was the great thing when it was brought in. Jim James and I headed at a slow, careful walk around the field. Jeeps rolled past us raising clouds of white dust. Sunburned boys squatted in the shade of P-38's, watching us steadily but without comment or greeting. When we spoke to them they raised their fingers and murmured, "Hi."

I was on the watch for rocks to take home to Joan, who had displayed some interest in geology. A tall young man in a baseball cap and a pair of faded shorts was working on an electric generator and we stopped to talk. He said he came from Alabama and had been on Canton eight months. Two other boys came around the generator and looked at us curiously. One said he was from Oregon, the other said he was from Indiana and they were tentmates of the kid in the shorts. I told them I was looking for samples of rocks and they seemed to hesitate, finally invited us over to their tent to see their shell collections. Out of their trunks they took bags of round, brown shells which were polished until they looked as though they had been glazed. They spread them out on their cots, picking out the most perfect ones for us to admire. They eagerly presented me with a dozen or so. I thanked them and inquired what they did for amusement besides collecting shells. They said nothing, except go in swimming or see a movie when an old one was shipped out to the island. You had to be careful swimming, they said, because of snakes and also because of infections that got into coral cuts, sometimes got into your ears. There was a little excitement when the Japs came over but even that distraction was growing more infrequent.

I told the boy from Alabama I had some Honolulu newspapers and some old copies of *Time* in the plane and asked him if he would like them. He said, "Yeah, thanks," without great interest. We walked back to the plane. Alabama said he used to play a lot of basketball in high school. He would like to go home. He said hopelessly but without rancor that he guessed he was the forgotten man of this war. I gave him the magazines and the newspapers and he scuffed away slowly across the field.

We got back in the plane, wet with perspiration. A few minutes later we were shivering with cold, climbing into the air,

46

and the little white atoll of Canton had dropped out of sight beyond the hazy horizon.

We were flying almost exactly southwest along a rim of naval and air bases which stretched from Oahu to New Caledonia (see front end-paper map). In the spring of 1943 this was the outer edge of our frontier, which protected our shipping lanes and faced the opposing perimeter of the Jap's long line of ocean bases. The Jap was operating along interior lines: we were spread around a great concave circle inside of which we hoped to confine and ultimately crush him. It was into these bases that we had poured men and supplies. To places like Canton, Palmyra, Johnston, Viti Levu—islands of which few Americans had ever heard—we had sent shipload after shipload of construction equipment, ordnance, motor vehicles, to convert barren atolls and jungle-covered volcanic isles into a chain of tent cities and small forts which reached some 4000 miles around the globe. People wondered sourly what the Navy was doing in the months after December 7, 1941. That was one thing. It was a great undertaking; modern war cannot be waged without every one of all the multitudinous parts that go into the military engine. No matter how small the base, it requires its infinite detail of preparation, its quantity of sea-borne supplies, its machine shops, camouflage netting, distilleries, kitchens, sanitation equipment. It was no wonder that the Alabama basketball player had been overlooked.

Our next stop was to be Viti Levu, one of the Fiji group. We flew the rest of that morning and well into the afternoon, lunching on thin-sliced pieces of bologna between thick-sliced squares of dank bread which stuck to the roof of my mouth and rolled up into lumps the size of golf balls. James, Shrout, Cohn and I were initiated into the Short Snorters by Wolfert and a member of the crew—M. J. Cochran is the name on my bill. We came out of the clouds over Viti Levu, circled above coral reefs which looked like patches of green ink on the deep blue spread of the ocean, swooped over native sailing canoes, rain-soaked rice paddies, sugar cane fields, thatched bamboo huts, and sat down on the airfield. In my mind the Fiji Islands had always been a name synonymous with faraway romance, largely because of Phineas T. Barnum, I suppose. But a few

47

hours after we landed I ran into a young man named Arthur Tallaksen, of West Orange, New Jersey, which is only a few miles from where I was born. Such incongruities ceased to surprise me after a few months in the South Pacific but I was still impressed then.

It had been raining steadily for three days on Viti Levu. The airfield and the roads were deep in mud. A truck carted us to the transient officers' barracks, where we were to be billeted for the night while the crew of our plane got some rest. There we shaved and showered in cold water in a long wooden shed with a cement floor.

Ira had promoted a truck with a driver and a guide to take us into the nearby village of Nandi. It began to rain again as we skidded off along Viti Levu's narrow, winding roads, passing lush green fields, native huts and an occasional Fiji Islander, who returned our stares. I was glad to see that they wore sarongs and had fuzzy hair.

Nandi consisted of one muddy street across which roamed scrawny horses and cows undisturbed by our honking. Shops on both sides were built on an elevation to keep them out of the mud. Hindus in dirty white drapes swarmed around, regarding us with sly curiosity. The wares of the dark little shops could not be identified from the street, but one place sported a big sign which read: "Pop's Hamburger."

We got out and splashed through the wetness in the wake of our guide, Lieutenant E. S. Bridges, who came from South Carolina. Ira and I had told him we wanted to buy some silver. He took us into a shop. On one side was a counter covered with bowls of bright-colored, exotic-smelling spices. On the other side were ancient glass cases in which was displayed some silver filigree jewelry. The shop, like all the others, was lightless. The sudden tropic night was beginning to close down, but Hindu storekeepers could apparently see in the dark. We stood in the window holding the jewelry up against the fading light outside, squinting at it while we bargained. Prices were not cheap. The souvenir business in the South Pacific is a sellers' market. A lot of American soldiers and sailors have more money than they know what to do with.

Rain was still falling. By the time we got back to the bar-

48

racks it was teeming, so I was astonished to see men sitting on the long wooden benches of the camp's open-air movie theatre. Bridges said, "Sure, they sit through a movie in the rain." The show didn't start until seven o'clock. It was then only five-thirty. "They want to get good seats," the Lieutenant explained. Later in the evening I groped my way along a path past the theatre. It was filled with a silent crowd of soldiers. Rubber hats and raincoats glistened in the light thrown by the projector. Behind the curtain of rain was the large figure of Wendell Willkie. I paused long enough to discover that the picture was a news reel of Mr. Willkie's 1940 Presidential campaign.

Ruth Aust, whom I had met in Honolulu, had told me to look up Lieutenant Colonel C. F. Beyers if I got to Viti Levu. I phoned him from the ATC office and he came around in a reconnaissance car and carted James and me back to his quarters. Beyers and his chief, Colonel Harris, lived in a "bouri" which the natives had built for them. The roof was thatched and the walls were made of stripped bamboo tightly woven. The Harris-Beyer bouri was the snuggest thing I saw in the South Pacific.

Beyers, in the process of constructing camps and various installations, had had a great deal of business with native labor. The population of the Fijis, he said, was half native Polynesian, half Hindu. The latter had been brought in some years ago by private companies to work on the plantations. Beyers did not care for the Hindus. He said they were hot-headed and lazy. He liked the Fijians, however. Their labor market was controlled and had to be contracted for through district "kings." Negotiations always involved elaborate feasts and ceremonies, but after the proper arrangements had been made there was no more trouble. The kings delivered.

I asked Beyers how the soldiers got along in the Fijis and how they liked it. He said they were bored because there was not much in the way of amusement outside of the movies. Organized sports were impractical because military duties were always intervening. The men could go sightseeing but the novelty of the country soon wore off. Some of the Polynesian girls were quite pretty. The enlisted men were allowed six cans of beer a week. The officers could get gin, rum or brandy at the officers' club, but most of the liquor was Australian and pretty bad. To prove it he brought out a bottle of rum which nearly took the tops of our heads off.

He said the climate was healthy and temperate though, about the same as Honolulu's. There was no malaria but you had to be careful not to be bitten by certain species of the great variety of insects, reptiles and small mammals which swarmed around. A tiny toad was hopping across the floor of the Colonel's bouri and he told us that this particular creature could lather itself up with a venomous foam which was instantly fatal to dogs or any of the toad's enemies that happened to lick it. We fortified ourselves with another shot of the Colonel's terrible rum.

I told the Colonel about the boys James and I had run into at Canton. I said that I had also noticed among the soldiers and young officers around Viti Levu a kind of lifelessness that was hardly typical of Americans of their age. There was not much swagger in them. They were even shy, though they seemed to be almost pathetically eager to talk to newcomers. I asked if it was tropic duty that took the vinegar out of them. Beyers said he thought it did—tropic duty and inaction. When they had a chance to go into action they displayed plenty of vinegar. He said a curious phenomenon which he had noticed was the profuse way his men bled when they were cut. "They bleed like stuck pigs," he said. He had no explanation except that it might be from some deficiency in their diet.

Colonel Harris came in, swearing and shaking the rain off his hat. Over the rum we decided that someone had to hold down these island bases. Viti Levu was one of the links in our Pacific chain.

I was impressed by the strength of our installations there. But it also occurred to me that if the Japs had capitalized on time as we had to build up their bases, the island-by-island road to Tokyo was going to be arduous and sanguinary.

Beyers taxied us back to the barracks. My cot was the last one in a long row in an open building which had no protection along its sides but screens. The rain had sifted in and the head of my cot was soaked. While a score of other occupants snored on, unconcerned, I profanely rearranged the sheets so that the head was at the other end, crawled under a dank mosquito netting and slept with wet feet.

We were awakened at four-thirty. Our pilot had a real estate proposition cooking in San Francisco and was in a hurry to deliver his freight, get back and close the deal. It had stopped raining but it was dismally dark and everything smelled and felt wet. Breakfast was ready at the officers' mess—apples, hot cakes, scalding coffee. A few passengers and a number of ATC crews flying their planes out that morning sat at the long board table, looking sleepy, unshaven and aged. A few of the flyers finished and drifted into the lounge where they sprawled in wicker chairs playing poker while they waited for their colleagues. The flyers are the bigtime Charleys of the gambling in the Pacific. I made it a rule never to sit in a game with any of them. They tossed twenty-dollar bills around the way I toss nickels.

Towards cash-money the men in the services, particularly the young soldiers, have developed a kind of innocent contempt. Money, I found, could be left around with only a slight chance that it would be stolen, where watches, soap, razors, flashlights, trench coats, even jeeps would vanish while you turned your head. The soldier gambled for distraction and because it was something for his money to do. There was almost nothing it could be spent for. Cigarettes cost sixty cents a carton at the canteens and other items such as candy, shaving cream, toothpaste were scaled down in comparison. Food, clothing and living quarters were provided. A soldier's wages were gravy, which he casually tossed into the pot. Professional gamblers undoubtedly exploited this creamy situation. So did shrewd amateurs. One lieutenant sent home $500 which he made playing poker on the way to the South Pacific from San Francisco by boat. This was not an unusual take. But the lieutenant's games were just friendly ones, he said, for modest stakes. The games among the flyers, according to all the hearsay, would curl a conservative man's hair.

We loaded ourselves into trucks and jounced out to the field, stopping first at "Weather," then at "Operations" for pilots and navigators to get last-minute information and instructions. Our plane was already warming up and we got aboard, carrying big clots of Fiji mud with us on our shoes. We took off in the darkness at six o'clock Fiji time and flew into more clouds, more rain.

I had ceased to marvel at our magic-carpet progress, although in a little more than eighteen hours' flying time we had come 3400 miles. I had become indifferent to the thousands of miles of ocean below us and had forgotten all the briefing in the use of rubber rafts. Our land plane, which would not have floated thirty seconds if we had had to come down, lumbered along monotonously, its engines snoring, its minor noises of vibrations never varying. We read, we slept, we choked over more sandwiches, we looked down on the world with the contempt of modern man.

The crew, I presume, had a different attitude and paid attention to their chores. But we had long since become bored. We took for granted each miraculous, unerring hop across the world. I think we gave the navigator some credit by remarking casually now and then: "Marvelous the way he hits these little islands right on the nose." We didn't even bother to think what an infinitesimal error in his calculations would have meant to us, our families, even our firms.

I was much more concerned over a small disaster which overtook me in New Caledonia. Men from our office going off on a war assignment always provided themselves with a trench coat. A trench coat was the war correspondent's caparison. Dave Hulburd, head of our News Bureau and the man called upon to O.K. such purchases, laughingly referred to himself as Hart, Schaffner & Hulburd. My coat had come from Abercrombie & Fitch and was a cherished item in my gear.

When we dropped down on an airfield at the northern end of New Caledonia and disembarked I had the coat over my arm. We were to change planes. The C-87 was going on to Australia with its freight and Art Cohn. The rest of us would catch a plane going south along the New Caledonia coast to Tontouta.

Our gear was loaded on a truck. I placed the trench coat on top of my bag and we got in a jeep. Why we did never became clear. There was some confusion of orders and the jeep driver drove us across the red, muddy landing strip to an

Operations office, where a sergeant asked, "What do you want here?" If we intended to get to Noumea that afternoon we better hurry back on the field and grab a transport plane which was just about ready to take off. It was the last plane south that day. We jolted back, our driver mumbling bitterly that nobody ever knew what the hell was going on, and got there as they were getting ready to close the transport's door. We piled aboard and the truck with our gear backed around and our stuff was heaved in after us. The transport took off while we breathed hard and braced ourselves. This plane, a DC-3 in private life, was stripped down for war. There were no reclining seats, just a row of tin benches along each side with depressions in them like shallow wash basins for a man's posterior. We had been five or ten minutes in the air when I thought to check over my gear and discovered that the Abercrombie & Fitch coat had not been put aboard.

I grumped about it all the way to Tontouta and was probably not even gracious to a staff sergeant who had been in the other war and had an autograph book which he asked me to sign. He showed me a picture of his wife too. When we got to Tontouta I gave the pilot a note to take back requesting that my coat be forwarded to the Navy Press Relations Office in Noumea. I scarcely expected to see it again. I never did. I considered the affair a piece of outrageous carelessness, if not downright larceny, and was so annoyed that I forgot all about landing safe and sound on the other side of 4500 miles of sea.

As a matter of fact, we were still thirty or forty miles from Noumea and the most hair-raising part of the trip was still ahead. It was by Navy bus over a winding mountainous road. The bus was a truck with benches along the sides. We sat with our baggage piled between us, clutching whatever came to hand. We only got glimpses of the road ahead over the shoulder of the driver. But behind us we could watch the road streaking out, gyrating like a tail over eucalyptus-crowned hills, along the edges of cliffs and around blind curves. Trucks in almost solid line wooshed past us going the other way. Around curves, cliffs, up and down precipitous grades, the drivers never seemed to slacken speed. Natives with orange-colored hair standing on end, leaped out of our way. Frenchmen in European jalopies hugged the edges of the narrow highway and let the uproarious military traffic sweep by. An infantryman told me later that there was a special graveyard in New Caledonia for Navy truck drivers. I never confirmed the story but I believe it.

We finally hurtled past a big nickel works on a blue harbor's shore. Beyond were warships of the Pacific Fleet. We drove past ornate, unkempt little houses and into a town. Jeeps cluttered the narrow streets. Outside a white-walled building a marine in sun helmet stood guard. Before a pink-walled building a Frenchman in a visored cap carrying a bayoneted rifle walked his patrol. Coffee-colored Javanese, black Melanesians, little French girls in wide-brimmed straw hats, boys in shorts, sailors, Navy officers, picked their way along muddy, unpaved sidewalks. This was Noumea.

VII

TASK FORCE NORTH

To MY GREAT JOY there was a small stack of mail for me at the Navy Public Relations Office.

Peg had written daily. I searched her letters for signs of faltering courage. Joe the postman kidded her for being anxious about his arrival these days. She "read and reread" my letters. But those were the only hints of any anxiety. She wrote as though I were in the next town and poured out all the trivial, commonplace and precious news.

Her letters went back to May 5. The New Jersey suburbs had been perspiring in unseasonable heat—eighty-five in the shade. She had been to a bridge party and though she hadn't played for a long time and didn't care much about bridge, had won first prize—four perennial plants. The twins had had permanents. Joan had not been sure how she was going to like it and had let Susan have the first appointment with the hairdresser so she could study the effect. She decided that Susan looked all right and now they were both curled. They and their fellow Girl Scouts had been circularizing the town with warnings to people not to discuss troop movements. Joan was practicing daily on her violin for the Junior High School orchestra concert. Susan was practicing on her clarinet to march with the school band in the Memorial Day parade. Nancy was practicing on the piano for a Red Cross benefit recital.

Peg, between leading her Girl Scout troop, helping at the local Ration Board, running the house and listening to the cacophony of music, struggled with the meat and potato shortage: "We are having meat trouble, although the new ceiling prices are supposed to solve everything. There is no solution to the potato shortage. We've had none for nearly two weeks."

The girls were going to mow the lawn but she spotted "a marvelous crop of dandelions" and told them to wait until she had dug them up. She was paying twenty-five cents a pound for dandelion greens at the store. She was not driving the car any more than she could help because she was trying to save enough gas coupons to drive to Maryland. All year we looked forward to the two summer months which we spent at Oxford, Maryland. We had a house on Jack's Point on the shore of Town Creek, where wild ducks and herons paddle around the marshes and crabbers' boats chug lazily back and forth along their "trot" lines and the sun going down behind Wiley's boat yard is one of the lovely sights in the world.

Peg wrote that she had had a scare one night when she was listening to the Army hour on the radio and a sepulchral voice warned people on the East Coast that the danger of air raids was not over. Hitler was growing desperate. She was suddenly startled by the sound of shots, ran around the house and finally into the kitchen, where eight eggs which she had put on the stove to hardboil, and had forgotten, had exploded in a dry pan. "I should know by this time (after almost 17 years of marriage) how to boil eggs." She lamented that her letters were "silly," but only dull things seemed to happen at home.

It is remarkable how women who can imagine anything in the lonely hours of nighttime—except how commonplace and secure most of the daily life overseas actually is—can write thousands of words to their men without betraying themselves.

The Quonset hut which housed the Navy PRO was also the working headquarters of the newspaper correspondents in the South Pacific. The hut squatted in the muddy yard in front of a French school. Among the newsmen who welcomed us were Joe Driscoll of the *New York Herald Tribune,* Leif Erickson of A.P., George Jones of U.P., Jack Mahon of the *New York Daily News,* Gordon Walker of the *Christian Science Monitor.* There were also representatives of Australian and London newspapers. If the South Pacific was not in the news just then it was not because of lack of coverage. At long, littered wooden tables the correspondents pecked at their typewriters, read each other's dispatches in out-of-date papers and exchanged rumor, gossip and some facts. It looked and sounded like any city hall press room except here the newsmen were in uniform, albeit a heterogeneous collection of uniforms of which no two were alike. The current behind-the-hand gossip was that a major operation was cooking in the Solomons.

Noumea was one of the Navy's major bases of operations. It lay on the eastern rim of the Coral Sea and commanded the southern entrance to those waters. Westward was the coast of Australia. Above Noumea, like steppingstones around the sea's rim were the island groups of the New Hebrides, Santa Cruz and the Solomons.

The United States had first crept up the steppingstones onto the Solomons on August 7, 1942, when the Marines landed on Guadalcanal. Since then we had taken another short, tentative step forward onto Russell Island. But 100 miles above Russell, the Japs perched firmly on the island of New Georgia, and their submarines and aircraft still hunted across the Coral Sea, which was our supply route from Noumea. Our difficulties could be appreciated when it was realized that Noumea, itself dangling at the end of a 5400-mile ocean supply line was still some 1150 miles from our hard-pressed Solomon bases—more than half the distance from Los Angeles to Hawaii.

For almost a year we had been able to turn back the persistent counter-thrusts of the Japanese air and naval forces—no more. With the forces available in the Pacific we had been grimly holding on, building up our strength for the next step.

That step was now imminent. But "imminent" meant a month or more. Meanwhile it was possible to cover developments from here, attending the daily press interviews with Captain Ray Thurber, then Admiral Halsey's Chief of Staff, and sending stories via Radio Noumea.

I went into the office which the PRO Lieutenant Tom Lambert and his man Friday, Yeoman Bowman, occupied in the hut's rear. I teetered back in a folding canvas chair and asked for advice. I told Lambert, who was holding down the job while his boss, Lieutenant Commander Jim Bassett was on leave, I had no definite plans but that I would prefer to see some action rather than sit around here. My assignment was not to cover the Pacific war with daily stories. I was supposed to drift around and get the feel. I asked Lambert if he would put me aboard a warship until the time was ripe to move up to Guadalcanal. I would have liked a battleship or a carrier since they looked big and comfortable and comparatively safe. The trouble was I might sit out in the harbor for weeks and then see nothing but some routine maneuvers, Lambert explained, and suggested a "can"—a destroyer. He said he thought he could get me assigned to one almost immediately. I said, "O.K." and a can it was. A few minutes later, after some telephoning, he announced that I could probably go aboard one the following afternoon. Things moved fast out here.

We new arrivals spent that night at the Naval Receiving Station, which was a colony of Quonset huts built on the side of a hill just outside town. Tom Lambert drove us out in a jeep. A large part of a PRO's job on a war front is wet-nursing correspondents. The hut was full of naval officers en route somewhere, all of them about as bewildered as I was. I overhauled my gear. I had a large bundle of dirty clothes by now and not the faintest idea how to get them laundered so I decided to make a bundle of them and leave them until I got back.

My assignment to a destroyer was made definite the next morning. I left my bagful of dirty laundry in a corner of the PRO hut on top of a great pile of other bags and sacks belonging to other correspondents who were somewhere in the South Pacific and got in the PRO jeep. Lambert drove me to the waterfront. He had rounded up a fancy captain's gig. The cushions were swathed in white linen and I tried to keep my muddy GI shoes off them as I was transported across the harbor. I was certainly starting out to cover the war in plenty of style.

The Officer of the Deck received me courteously at the destroyer's rail and escorted me to the quarters of the skipper. Captain Schulz greeted me cordially although it was apparent that he was preoccupied with some other matter. He was in a state of exaltation and kept striding around, patting his Executive Officer, Lieutenant Commander Alfred White, and reading and folding and opening to read again an official-looking letter which had just been delivered to him. It developed that he had been transferred to shore duty after five years at sea. I thought to myself that he would be whistling a different tune after a few weeks in Washington, where he was going, but there was no point in spoiling his anticipation. All the officers I had run into in Washington wanted to go to sea. White was to have the ship so they were chuckling and grinning and congratulating each other. They suddenly remembered me. I was to sleep in the Exec's cabin, they said. They were glad to have me aboard. Right now we were all going ashore and have a drink to celebrate Schulz's and White's change of fortunes. We were not due to sail until the morning.

The three of us and Lieutenant (jg) John Fitzgerald taxied ashore in Schulz's launch. I gave my overseas cap a tilt, feeling like an officer, and we swaggered up to the Officers' Club in what used to be the Hotel Pacifique on the Noumea waterfront. Except for a meagre sprinkling of exceptionally homely nurses and Red Cross workers it was an all-male crowd, chiefly Navy men from the warships in the harbor. Staff men and other shore-based officers had their own clubs. It took a person with a long reach, like Schulz, to get a drink. They stood around the bar three-deep and overflowed into the garden outside. There was a good deal of loud, cheerful talk and the usual "scuttlebutt." This was a South Pacific rendezvous of the men who commanded the Pacific Fleet. For a lot of them the afternoon was a last chance to lift one before a long, dry spell at sea. Liquor and beer are taboo on Navy ships. For some of them it would turn out to be the last time ever. After eighteen months of a desperately fought naval campaign a lot of their colleagues were missing from this rendezvous.

In a mixture of Martinis and Tom Collinses—all the bar had was beer and gin—we drank to Schulz's new job and White's new ship. We went back to the landing, I surveying the world with the imperious eye of an admiral by now. Evidently a number of ships were preparing to move out the next morning. The landing swarmed with returning officers and men. A few of the sailors had misjudged their capacity for fun or had run afoul of the rotgut which the natives manufactured and bootlegged. They were sprawled on the shore. Their barges arrived at the big T-shaped pontoon dock and their shipmates picked them up by head and heels and heaved them aboard.

We had dinner in the destroyer's wardroom and on the

fantail afterwards watched a movie show. The night was dark except for searchlights streaking across the sky and blinker signals chattering silently from ship to ship and ship to shore. All around us in the harbor on the fantails of other warships the U.S. Navy sat absorbed in movies. A dance band on the sound track of a neighboring destroyer broke into the throbbing voice of Bette Davis, who was fluttering across our screen, suffering interminably under a domineering mother. I was more interested in the audience than the show. The officers sat in chairs, almost close enough to the screen to touch it. The men hung like monkeys on the five-inch guns and the superstructure behind us. They watched for the most part in interested silence, although at one point in Bette's agony of indecision over what to do with mother a hoarse voice shouted, "Aw, kill the old bitch!"

The show was over. The crew was ordered to stand fast. Schulz, towering against the blank canvas screen, faced his stocky Executive Officer and made a brief speech. "This is the best goddam destroyer in the fleet," said he. "I am proud of you." Then he read his dry orders from Washington. White read his, notifying him that he was to take command. "You are relieved, sir," he said to Schulz, and that was that.

In the darkness Fitz convoyed me safely around the clutter of gear, depth charges, anti-aircraft guns on the little ship's deck and left me in the Executive Officer's cabin forward. My cabinmate, the new Exec, came in. He was Lieutenant Donald Francis Quigley of Council Bluffs, Iowa. Until a few minutes ago, Red Quigley, age 25, Annapolis '41, had been chief engineer. I climbed into the upper berth and went to sleep.

At daybreak the next morning we were under way.

We threaded the harbor. We passed slowly under the rearing mountains of New Caledonia, which were innocent enough with green mantles hiding their gun emplacements. A village of tents and Quonset huts built on the face of a hill looked at a distance like a boy scout summer encampment in the Adirondacks. The harbor wound like a river through the hills, crowded with ships and sown with mines which we were anxiously careful to miss. Where the harbor widened out to the ocean there were hidden shoals, White told me, and he pointed

60

out a cargo ship which had run aground and now, gaunt and abandoned, was slowly breaking up. There were a number of other lean destroyers in our task force. A "task force" is a force of warships, any size, assigned to any task. Our assignment, White told me, was to take a convoy north. Our small herd which finally separated itself from the rest of the harbor shipping consisted of a number of other destroyers, two transports, a tanker and an old four-stack destroyer which, like most of her sisters, had been converted to transport use. The decks of the transports were brown with men. We were a fairly important force standing out to sea, heading north for Guadalcanal. We were a brave show.

Beyond the Noumea light we took our position and began the routine of zigzagging. Our Can was in the lead. We were under the enemy's guns, as it were, the moment we stuck our noses out. Japanese submarines had been active in the Coral Sea in recent weeks and every hour of our progress north brought us closer within the range of the Jap's aircraft.

Ours was a one-dimensional operation and therefore restricted in attack or defense. The enemy could attack us on the surface, undersea, in the air. But I had no great sense of danger that morning. To me it seemed more like a summer cruise in Long Island Sound. The sea was calm, the sky, blue.

I spent the morning on the bridge. White paced restlessly around, hands in pockets, shoulders hunched, approving orders with an "Aye, aye," in a casual voice. It was only when he stood making a silent, preoccupied study of the sea and the other ships that he betrayed any of the concern which he must have felt. It was his first command. Quigley monkeyed incessantly with the charts, moving the protractor and biting his nails. Officers and petty officers kept taking bearings on the New Caledonia shore and on the other vessels. Gunners sat beside the 20-millimeter anti-aircraft guns, taking turns at peering through glasses, which were mounted on sky lookouts so that no section of the sky escaped search. In protected cells, surrounded by instruments and dials, sound detector men watched and listened. I began to comprehend these operations later on. It was no summer cruise. We were stalking up the coast like a cat, back up, claws bared.

VIII

THE CAN

W<small>E BEGAN TO ROLL.</small> Two newly assigned ensigns got seasick. The sea was not high but we bucketed around like a porpoise, splashing spray along our decks so that frequently the only dry place was the navigating bridge. The motion was never the same for very long since we kept zigzagging, sometimes had the sea on our side, sometimes went charging squarely into it. An officer told me that battleship men have no appreciation of the life of a destroyer man, and destroyer men, I soon discovered, had nothing but disdain for life aboard a battlewagon. Our Can was some 340 feet long with about 34 feet beam, which is not much beam for stability. Into that space were packed—besides the 20-millimeter automatics—the four five-inch guns of our main battery, sixteen torpedo tubes in four quadruple mounts, depth charge racks and projectors, instruments, controls, engines, generators, winches, fuel, ammunition, stores, supplies, a hospital, a dispensary, galleys, pantries, laundry, and places for more than 200 men to sleep.

They placed me as the guest of honor on the right hand of Red Quigley, who occupied the head of the table at the officers' mess. White seldom came down to the wardroom for meals. He ate on the bridge and slept on a couch in the emergency cabin within earshot of the constant imbecilic chirp of the instruments. The officers were polite and even deferential. Outside of a few veteran chief petty officers, who had their own, separate mess, I was the oldest man forward of the break of the bridge; for that matter, older than 99 per cent of all the men aboard. The fact appalled me. I had always thought of myself as a young man up to this point.

The personnel of our Can was typical of the Navy's de-

62

stroyer fleet. White, who had graduated from Annapolis in 1929, was 37, my junior by a year. Quigley was 25. Fitzgerald was 24. Fitz's assistant, Lieutenant (jg) Bert Thompson, was 22. Out of fifteen officers these four were the only Academy men. The rest were "ninety day wonders," which should not be taken as a term of contempt. They had served a thirty-day apprenticeship as seamen, then had trained three months as midshipmen. With commissions as ensigns they had thereupon been sent out to the South Pacific. Most of them were university graduates who had taken a wide detour from their planned careers. Morris Zaritsky was studying medicine at the University of Pennsylvania when America went to war. Zaritz, who lived in Passaic, New Jersey, joined the Navy, went off to *Prairie State* training school and when they asked for volunteers for the engine room good naturedly put his hand up though he had no particular hankering for it. Now Zaritz, who was 22 and a few years ago intended to be a doctor, had been moved into Quigley's old birth; he was our Can's chief engineer. His assistant was 24-year-old Eugene Cox, who had graduated from Southern Cal in 1939.

The ship's doctor, Lieutenant Henry Moore, was 27. The Doc, a tall sardonic man, had been a pediatrician in private life, which I thought was amusing considering the youthfulness of the men now in his care. But the wardroom was too serious about its job to be kidded on this score. I never alluded to it, even after we got better acquainted. These youngsters who had gone to such schools as Northwestern, Georgia Tech, Michigan, Southern California, intending to be peaceful civilians, turned out to be amazingly competent at this new game. This was the generation that was supposed to be a washout.

Those who were wise leaned on the chief petty officers for technical aid and advice. The CPO's, who were up from the ranks, are the backbone of the Navy as the sergeants are the backbone of the Army. Before the war an enlisted man had little chance of rising beyond a chief's rank. Between these old-timers and the new ninety-day officers who had become their immediate superiors, existed a peculiar relationship which depended on tolerance and tact. The Navy's justification of the system was to be found somewhere in the old Navy tradition

63

that an officer was also a gentleman. Because of wartime necessity a lot of CPO's now have been given commissions. The old hierarchy of Annapolis still rules the top roosts, but on the lower rungs the Academy men have been spread thinner and thinner through our expanding fleets.

White told me that except for the decoding room I could have the run of the ship. But there were few places to run and even fewer to sit down. Outside of the wardroom, which the Negro messmen were always scrubbing or painting, Red's and my small cabin, which had room enough for just one straight-back chair, there was no place for a man to get down on the small of his back and put his feet in the air. The bridge had two pivoting stools to sit on, and the signal flag box. I spent the afternoon wandering around. The rolling ocean was peaceful, the blue sky was bland. But in these waters the *Lexington* and one, possibly three enemy carriers had gone down in a five-day combat in June, 1942, the first carrier versus carrier engagement of the war.

Night dropped like a curtain and we were blacked out. Nighttime brought uneasiness. I thought I had learned the route from my cabin up to the bridge but when I tried it I collided with stanchions, groped, slid my feet forward inches at a time. I thought I never would find the inclined ladders which led on high. I stayed on the bridge until around ten o'clock, in a restless, suspenseful world where even the stars were strange. I had something of a shock when I looked into the heavens and could not find the North Star. It was the first time I realized that Polaris dropped out of sight below the Equator. Astern of us was the mariner's guide in this part of the world—the Southern Cross.

Ahead of us was a dark horizon, and over it somewhere, the enemy. The enemy might be in the dark water around us too. I tried to imagine the lighted interior of a submarine below the waves and Japanese officers hissing orders and listening at their instruments and moving their controls. But the notion seemed too utterly fantastic. That is one difficulty about comprehending modern war. Most of it is fantastic. I could not even comprehend that a peaceful man like myself was running the chance of sudden and violent death from enemy action.

64

I groped my way back to my cabin, able to see a little better now that my eyes were accustomed to the darkness. I hung my clothes in a careful sequence, arranging my shoes, helmet and life jacket beside them so that if General Quarters sounded during the night I could get quickly and properly dressed.

G.Q. helmets and life jackets were *de rigueur*. Red had told me that they always had a routine General Quarters in the morning, but I need not turn out for it if I didn't want to, he said. One of the stewards would come around and wake Red a few minutes beforehand. Red liked to grab a cup of coffee before he reported on the bridge. I made a mental note to wait and see how I felt in the morning before making any decisions.

I put thoughts of enemy submarines out of my mind and went to sleep. The next thing I knew the steward was waking us. I could not move. While Red crawled out below me, dressed and went out, I pretended to be asleep, feeling very sorry for my cabinmate. I had dozed off again when a loud squawk brought me up so suddenly that I cracked my head on the overhead. The squawk kept up, over and over, imperative, insistent, a little terrifying. Feet clumped alongside the narrow passageway and men brushed against the curtain hanging in the doorway. I heard Lieutenant Whittaker, the paymaster, come out of the room across from mine. The iron door leading out to the weather deck kept clanging and rattling as men whirled the big wheel that opened it, pushed it closed and secured it again. The dull roar of the blower in the cabin faded out, stopped. There was the silence of a tomb in the officers' country. I felt very lonesome. The cabin began to grow stuffy. It occurred to me that if there were an attack now I would have no warning; the ship was already at General Quarters and everyone was at his fighting station. But it would be undignified to appear now, late, blinking foolishly through my spectacles from under my tin helmet. I weighed uneasiness against dignity and dignifiedly drifted back to sleep. I was relieved though when I heard the officers returning and knew that they had "secured from G.Q." I looked at my watch. It was going on chow time, so I got up. But I resolved that hereafter G.Q.

would find me on deck helmeted and alert, not all alone below in pajamas.

Gradually in the days and nights that followed I sorted out, somewhat, the complexities of life going on around me. I was impressed with the terrible efficiency of this rolling, bucking mechanism of destruction. Almost every motion a man made became virtually automatic; in the stress of battle terror might rob a man of his ability to think. As we zigzagged steadily north, still with no alarms, I watched the machinery of destroyer life as it ticked on, set to explode in a split second. We were a spear without a shield. Our thin skin would hardly stop a 50-calibre bullet. Our defense was offense. While the ordinary business of sailing and navigating the ship went on and the other vessels in our task force plowed along behind us, shifting position, talking to us with signal flags or over the TBS (radio telephone between ships), our Can constantly rehearsed for combat.

"Talkers" with telephones strapped around their sunburned necks relayed mock orders between the bridge and the gun director. I listened to the nerve system which enabled our Can to react with the swiftness of a cat:

The Bridge—"Contact, range nine-oh-double-oh, bearing one-zero-eight degrees true."

The Director—"Contact range eight-oh-five-oh bearing one-zero-five degrees true."

The Bridge—"Aye."

The Director—"Target course two-six-three degrees true, speed two-oh . . . range six-seven-double-oh bearing one-zero-four . . . target changing course to the right."

The Bridge—"Firing torpedoes. . . . Prepare to illuminate with star shells . . . illuminate."

I watched the torpedo men, riding quadruple tubes, swing their mounts out, pointing the projectiles over the side. I watched gun turrets swing, gun snouts rising and falling and twitching like massive cat's whiskers.

I watched loaders practice at loading machines on deck, lifting out dummy five-inch shell cases, passing them, shoving them home with a great rackety-clackety-clack.

It was not all work. Off watch there was time to read, sit

66

around and sing to a guitar under the lee of the after deck house, write "sugar reports" (which are letters to your girl), and shoot the breeze. A favorite topic among the crew was Sydney, Australia. Our Can had spent some time in convoy duty along the Australian west coast. Any one of the crew, at the drop of a hat, would talk about Sydney. They considered themselves connoisseurs of Sydney girls. One of them wanted to go back there, marry and settle down. But the favorite topic was the United States.

They were angry over stories of strikes. Among the crew were boys from labor union backgrounds. I suggested to them that radio news reports, mimeographed and distributed every morning, exaggerated the seriousness of labor troubles in America. One boy said, "Yeh, I know damn well how the radio and the kept press play labor news. I know management is to blame for it if it is bad. I know my old man wouldn't walk out unless he had good reason. He never thought I amounted to a hell of a lot but he looked pretty bad when I left to enlist. He knows I'm out here in the Navy. He works at Flint. He wouldn't walk out without he had damn good reason, would he? Would he, do you think?"

The officers' views were sharper. They'd hang that so-and-so Lewis for treason, they said. They shook their heads over labor. They laid claim to a pretty cosmopolitan outlook, now that they had seen Australia, and they talked about Australian labor, which they said behaved worse than American. Australian labor struck for holidays, sometimes for various reasons refused to unload ships carrying war supplies, and was pretty indifferent to the war effort, according to them. They thought it was significant that Australia had a labor government. To what degree their opinions were justified was arguable and for the sake of exploration I argued. But a point beyond debate was the extent to which their opinions had become fixed. I found out in time that the same views were prevalent among Navy and Army officers all over the South Pacific.

Over and beyond their anger and perplexity at some of the reports they got from the faraway "states side," was an unquestioning faith in the future. They were sure that their civilian life was going to pick up again at approximately the point it left off. The chance to return to that life was the main thing they were fighting for. They had reassuring letters from back home. "Dear Pete—How are you getting along? Don't you worry about the job. It will be right here waiting for you when you come back. . . ." Pete, who was now a mess attendant in the crew's galley, used to be a truck driver on a Texas oil field. After the war was over, Pete was going home with the letter in his wallet. And Pete's girl would wait. Pete was sure of that. "Mom is always writing me that my girl never goes out with no one only other girls."

We decided in the wardroom one night that the United States was going to have to police the world. How, the officers were not sure. But somehow the United States was going to have to do it.

They were an ordinary crowd of American boys, sober and thoughtless, ambitious and lazy, good and bad. The crew in helmets and lifejackets looked heroic at their battle stations. Doing routine jobs, standing in chow lines, lounging around off watch, they looked like a nondescript gang of American farmhands or factory workers. They were tough or they wouldn't have been able to stand destroyer life. Frequently they were unshaven, though a lot of them were just growing their first fuzz. They handled machinery with the familiarity and competence that is characteristic of their generation. Outside of their wrath over organized labor they had no political views of any account. They talked hard, their conversations full of obscenities. Alone, they were shy, naïve and sentimental, and showed me albums and letters and pictures of their girls. Occasionally they were insubordinate. Occasionally they transgressed one of the other many rules of Navy conduct.

I asked the new skipper how he punished them. He admitted that it was a problem. The ship was so crowded there was no room for a brig. Besides, every man aboard was needed at his job. To confine a man meant losing two hands—the miscreant and another man to guard him. Giving a man a dishonorable discharge meant giving him a ticket back to the States. There were some who figured that was O.K. no matter what the circumstances. Assigning them unpleasant jobs was no good solution either because some of the unpleasantest jobs had to be performed by responsible men. Money meant very little to them, but a fine was the usual sentence in a minor case.

The minor cases were handled by a Summary Court-martial: three officers and a judge advocate. The offender had the right to ask for counsel. Few of them did. I watched a trial. The judge advocate, Bert Thompson, the most boyish-looking man in the wardroom, looked a little self-conscious. But he and the court followed the proceedings as laid out in the book and conducted the case with a solemnity which had a certain effect on the gulping culprit. He had been caught sleeping on watch. Behind the court, as he well knew, stood the captain, the commander of the task force, the admiral of the fleet and the Judge Advocate General in Washington. He was being tried, in fact, not by several rather embarrassed boys of his own age but by the U.S. Navy.

A General Court-martial, consisting of twelve officers, could be summoned for more serious offenses. A General Court-martial could mete out a sentence of death.

I think the chief factor in maintaining good behavior was everyone's awareness of his responsibility in keeping their world afloat. It was a matter of survival. And as a man grew into his job his awareness became also a matter of devotion. He became a part of the ship.

The convoy crept on across the treacherously peaceful Coral Sea. Zaritz pridefully took me down into his engine room, which I admired, thinking all the time of the possibility of a torpedo exploding in these eerie compartments. I was happy to get out on deck again. As we emerged from a hatch, a wave swept over and drenched us. Fitz took me proudly into No. 2 gun turret and through the manholes down a trunk into the powder magazines. Here in the bottom of the ship was the lower handling room, where shells were passed from the magazine and loaded onto hoists which jerked them aloft to the gun turret. The men who had these stations worked surrounded by thousands of pounds of dynamite. The hatches above them were always dogged down, Fitz said, to give some protection to men topsides from an explosion in the magazine. I didn't like this part of the ship either and I was glad to climb out.

69

Fitz told me the story of a Negro mess attendant whose battle station was in the lower handling room. Someone had given him a vivid description of another destroyer which had taken a torpedo in her magazine. Her whole bow and the men below had been blown to smithereens. Our Can had gone into action. The mess attendant was below with nothing to do now but pray for deliverance and pass the ammunition. Furiously he passed the shiny brass cases. He passed so fast that the gun crew above in No. 1 turret was able to put out 17 rounds in 20 seconds. Average rate of fire for a five-inch gun is 15 rounds a minute. Shells were coming up faster than the crew could load and fire. The turret was cluttered with unexploded shells, and minutes after the action was all over they were still erupting up from below. The crew hollered down to the mess attendant to belay, the action was over. "Fire 'em anyhow," he shouted back hoarsely. "Ah ain't got no use for 'em down here."

I told Fitz how I felt about the station. He said hell, it was no more hazardous than any other station on a warship in combat.

The two ensigns stayed seasick, though they grimly stood their watches with buckets alongside. Their misery was silent and deep. The rest of us ate heartily and well and I had more proof that Navy men fare well at the table. Chief steward in the officers' mess was a Filipino, who also barbered the officers' heads. He told me while he was cutting mine that he had learned the trade in the last war when he was aboard a hospital ship. They wanted someone to barber the wounded and he had volunteered. Before he got through, he said, he was pretty good.

One of the mess attendants was a colored boy named Glover who fancied himself as a lady's man and owned a white skivvy shirt on which he had indelibly stencilled: "Glover the Lover." The pastry cook was a veteran named Madison. Madison was my man.

I praised some of Madison's cookies, which indeed were superior. I had no idea what I was starting though Red Quigley thought I had. Madison was inspired. The wardroom table at every meal was heaped now with Madison's baking. As Madison appeared proudly bearing some new creation, such as a five-

70

layer cake, Red eyed me knowingly. Red profited more than I did. He had a bigger appetite.

One of Madison's cakes was a legend. Madison had had his ups and downs and had served on several ships. He would climb laboriously up through the classes of cooks, slip, and have to start over again. Once he thought a new rating (a step up in rank) was coming to him but it failed to materialize. He brooded. He finally went into the galley and built a masterpiece of a cake. It had layer upon layer, with setbacks, and cornices and frescoes of icing. On top of it he wrote in pink on white icing: *No Rating—Why?*, set it down before the captain, and stood back to view the results. The results were not what Madison had anticipated. The pop-eyed captain ate a piece of cake, but it was a long time before Madison ever got his rating.

We were four days out of Noumea. We steamed past San Cristobal. The last streaks of a bloody sunset vanished and the horizon ahead of us turned dark. On the deck below the bridge I stood talking to Mr. Benjamin Franklin Hepburn and several other CPO's. Hepburn, a big beefy, grey-headed veteran, was Fire Control Chief. We talked about Guadalcanal, which lay just over the sightless horizon.

This was the first time that our Can had been in these waters in over a year and the CPO's understandably had their fingers crossed. They called the waters between Guadalcanal and Tulagi "Iron Bottom Bay." There were enough sunken ships in those waters to make a good-sized fleet—*Canberra, Astoria, Quincy, Vincennes, Atlanta, Juneau, Northampton*—all, except the Australian *Canberra,* American cruisers; at least nine American destroyers and one transport; two Japanese battleships, some seventeen Jap cruisers and destroyers and eight Jap transports. Uncounted thousands of men had perished in the sea, had died on the beaches and in the islands' jungles. You would almost expect the tropic stars to go out in such a malignant spot of the world. But the stars shone innocently on. And as we stood there, with the soft wind in our faces, I smelled a sweet and fleeting odor. I asked the chiefs if they could smell it. One of them lifted his nose and sniffed. "Oh, yeh," he said. "You can smell it even out here when the wind is right. That's Guadalcanal." The odor was the unmistakable fragrance of flowers.

IX

BATTLE OF THE BLIND

W E FOUGHT A NIGHT ENGAGEMENT up there a year ago,"
Hepburn said bitterly. "I don't want to be in another one
like that. That was the Battle of Savo Island on the night of
August 8." That fight was the climax of our Can's first eight
months in the war. Up to that time she had been plying between Honolulu and Australia and had not been scratched.
From fragments of conversations I had put together her brief
history, which is worth reciting because it is typical of the
little ships of the "Tin Can Fleet." They get no rest. They
perform every kind of mission—defend, strike, rescue, even
transport. They are sent in against enemy transports, submarines, cruisers, battleships. Some of our Can's sisters had
seen more action than she had. Many of them after 17 months
of war were at the bottom of the sea. The Navy had written
their epitaphs in brief communiques: *We lost one destroyer.*

Our Can was commissioned in 1937. A few days before December 7, 1941, she returned from a routine peacetime training
cruise, minced into Pearl and moored alongside Ford Island
not far from the *Utah*. I imagine her crew was thinking about
shore leave when the Japs appeared. Our Can ran like a scared
hen from hawks, trying to get out into the open sea. The Japs
were busy with the big fellows and she escaped unscathed.

She searched the Pacific for the Jap carrier force which
had launched the attack. Then she joined a carrier task force
for three weeks and finally put back into Pearl Harbor for a
rest. She was there less than twenty-four hours when she was
transferred to convoy duty. She headed south, escorting reinforcements and supplies for the island base of Canton.

Back in Pearl again she had two days to refurbish and refuel, then she hustled south in the carrier *Lexington*'s force, bound this time for the Coral Sea. On February 20, off Bougainville, the Japs spotted the force and attacked with twenty aircraft. That was the afternoon Butch O'Hare distinguished himself by tackling singlehanded a squadron of nine enemy bombers and shooting down five. As for our Can, something went wrong with her steering gear and she began to circle around and around, unable to help the *Lexington,* unable to use any evasive tactics to protect herself from falling bombs. Luckily she was not hit and the crew got the steering gear functioning again. The *Lexington* force, which had intended a sneak hit-run attack on Rabaul, turned tail after that. They were way off base, and having been located by the Japs, would be prey for land-based aircraft.

Our Can, in the midst of this streaming retreat, ran into another misfortune. She "wiped" a bearing. She signalled the task force commander her plight as she lost speed, and the commander wished her well, said good-bye and sped on. Our Can was not altogether in the expendable class but she was more expendable than the *Lexington* or any of the cruisers in the force.

The engine room crew went to work at scraping a new bearing and calibrating it to fit within one one-thousandth of an inch. While our Can struggled south at an agonizing five knots the anxious personnel searched the northern and western horizon beyond which lay the Jap bases on Bougainville. Gun crews stood at their stations as the hours crept by. Sound detector men listened tensely for the vibration that would mean the approach of an enemy submarine. For ten hours the engine room crew labored and our little Can wallowed helplessly in enemy-dominated waters.

But the Jap never appeared. The new bearing was finished and fitted into place. At full speed again our Can went streaking out of danger.

For several months after that she patrolled the supply lines around Australia until she was ordered back to Pearl and then, to the great joy of all hands—Mare Island for an overhaul. She was there three weeks, long enough for Red Quigley to get married. Red said good-bye to his new pretty wife (whose picture stood on Red's desk) and our Can headed west again for the war.

That was in the early summer. Our Can had been in constant service ever since, and when I came aboard she had been in the South Pacific a total of nearly seventeen months, averaging only five days in port out of every two months. The one frail hope of her personnel was that she might be sent back to Mare Island for a new piece of detector equipment. The equipment had been promised and involved some complicated installation. Everyone in the wardroom was concerned about this possibility but no one more so than Red. Since sailing from Mare Island he had become a father and his wife had sent him a picture of his daughter and a lock of her hair, a little silken ringlet which was as red as the proud Quigley's.

On August 7, 1942, our Can arrived off Guadalcanal with the force that was going to invade the Solomons. While the Marines were busy landing on Guadalcanal and Tulagi our Can and the other warships in the convoy took positions in the twenty-odd-mile-wide channel between to screen the transports and cargo ships from attack. The Japs made a fruitless bombing run that first afternoon. On the afternoon of the eighth they came back whooping—in forty torpedo and dive bombers, which were knocked down or chased off by American fighter planes and ships' ack-ack. The Japs succeeded, however, in setting fire to the 11,773-ton transport *George F. Elliot* (the ex-*City of Los Angeles*), and put a fish in the destroyer *Jarvis*.

The *Jarvis*, with a big hole in her bow, set out for home. Our Can had been with the *Jarvis* up and down the Pacific, in and out of port. Usually the two ships moored side by side. Our Can's officers and crew had many good friends aboard the *Jarvis*. They watched her go with misgivings. Even with night closing down, affording some cover, she would be running a dangerous gantlet, close to enemy airfields and roving Jap raiders. They noted that she was making little better than six knots. It was probably better to go back, however, than stay here. She limped north, intending to go around Cape Esperance at the top of Guadalcanal and creep south along the island's west coast. The waters off the island's east coast were not charted

74

then as they are now and were thought to be dangerous for deep-draft vessels. The *Jarvis* rounded the Cape.

Those events were the prelude to the Battle of Savo Island, the worst naval defeat the Navy has suffered since Pearl Harbor. The battle has been described, though never clearly. The eye-witness stories I picked up aboard our Can, fragmentary and unsatisfactory as all stories of a night naval engagement will always be, throw a little more light into that dark fiasco.

Our Can's captain, F. N. Walker then, had his worries that August afternoon. The operations so far had gone off too smoothly. Men were as nervous as cats. They were also tired after the strain of hours on end at battle stations when signal flags and blinkers relayed the ominous message that a Jap surface attack could be expected sometime that night. A strong enemy force was believed to be on the way down from Bougain-ville and should arrive in the early morning, probably around three o'clock. Walker got his little ship in readiness.

In a slugging match of the kind anticipated the destroyers' chief job would be to run interference for the cruisers, whose big guns would deliver the heavy blows. The Allied force was divided into two columns, one column being assigned to patrol along the Tulagi side of the channel, the other along Guadal-canal. At the entrance to the channel Savo Island sat like a hummock in a mill pond, dark and forlorn. Two destroyers took stations there, on either side, to pick up the first warning of the advancing Jap force and flash word to the cruisers and destroyers inside.

Walker had been assigned to the Guadalcanal side where he was to act as screen for the heavy Australian, *Canberra*. The Navy has released few details of the battle but it is known that on the Tulagi side were the American heavy cruisers *Astoria*, *Quincy*, and *Vincennes* with their screen of destroyers.

"It was a pitch-black night," one of the men told me. "There was a heavy overcast and to make matters worse a fine rain had begun to fall. I couldn't see a damn thing at my station. Looking into that night was like looking into a well. I located the ammunition drums by feel. The bridge knew where we were headed no doubt, but for all us guys could tell we might have been heading for Australia. Except we could tell by the

75

wake that we were running back and forth. We were wishing to hell we were heading for Australia. Waiting is what gets you down. You crap out before the shooting even starts."

On the dark bridge officers watched the faintly lighted dials of their instruments, eyed their luminous watches, listened to the harsh voices over the inter-ship radio speaking code-gibberish: "Sam from Pete—acknowledge." "Pete from Sam—Roger."

A nervous lieutenant wiped the wet lenses of the binoculars with which he had been studying the nighttime. Probably two hours yet before the Japs would arrive. He wished to hell he could go below and have a cup of coffee and smoke a cigarette. He might have been thinking of Sydney or Pearl Harbor or Golden Gate when the bridge, the gun turrets, anti-aircraft batteries, rails, stanchions, the whole ship and the stiff, surprised men aboard her leaped into view, suddenly illuminated by a searchlight out of the darkness which fell full upon them.

It was one of those occasions when men had to depend on reflexes set up by long rehearsals. In the terrible, betraying light the bridge spoke, talkers spoke, 20-millimeter automatic guns jerked and spoke, chattering, shattering the suspense, spewing tracers, until the eye of the light went out and the blackness wrapped them again. But the eye had found our Can and the *Canberra* too. There was a moment's breathless pause. The Gunnery Officer was spinning his dials, getting his solutions, training the main batteries of our Can. The foul night was cracked open again by the bark of her five-inch guns. At the same time, in the night's void flashed the enemy's batteries.

The water around our Can was shot full of geysers. In the after gun crew shelter, men swung the shells from the ammunition hoists into the breech of their gun with the same racket-clackety-clack as in practice. It was the last remembered sound. Some of the men didn't even remember that. A split second later they were mangled forms flung against the bulkhead, sprawled in the wreckage of the shelter. A Jap shell had hit and burst inside. Damage control crews, first aid men groped their way aft swearing in fright and anger. The after deck was no longer familiar. The scream of a wounded man cut through the ear-splitting bark of the guns. Men huddled around the wreckage of twisted steel plates. Three of their shipmates had been killed, ten wounded. They dragged them below into sick bay, Doc Moore's little white-lighted, sterilized cell. Miraculously the shell fragments had failed to detonate the magazine. Walker's ship was hurt but not mortally.

Fortunately for her she was not the enemy's main target. The Japs were after the big Australian and it was on her they turned the weight of their fire power. The men on our Can learned later that the enemy landed some of his first salvos on the *Canberra's* bridge, wounding her captain and disrupting her communications and controls. The *Canberra* was like a fighter hit in the face, momentarily blinded and paralyzed. Before she could recover, bursting shells had transformed her into a pyre. Reaching flames lighted her, made her a target into which the enemy continued to pour projectiles.

The action, which seemed interminable, had begun and ended in less time than it would have taken the nervous lieutenant to smoke his cigarette. How the Japs, arriving far ahead of the time they were expected, had escaped detection by the destroyers stationed off Savo has never been explained. Apparently they had slipped past the destroyer patrolling the western side as she was making her turn under the shore of Guadalcanal.

At any rate, there they were inside the channel. They swept past the dying *Canberra,* turned and headed towards Tulagi. According to various accounts, the American ships on the Tulagi side did not go into action until they were fired upon and wonderment has been expressed as to why they waited. The Navy has not disclosed its own analysis of the affair and writers have been left to reconstruct events and make their own speculations. It may have been that the ships in the other column were uncertain about the identity of friend and foe in the flashing of gunfire and the flickering of flame some eight or ten miles away in the black night.

Identification, difficult at first, became practically impossible in the subsequent confusion. The *Astoria,* steaming along behind the *Vincennes,* suddenly found herself illuminated by parachute flares dropped from a plane. A searchlight caught her fleetingly and shells began to straddle her and rain down on

77

her deck. Another searchlight pinned her from another quarter. She shot that one out but shells were landing on and all around her, knocking men out of the sky control, smashing her superstructure and starting fires that could not be quenched. She was pulverized and wrecked and staggered across the channel to burn to death.

The *Vincennes* underwent the same kind of onslaught. Torpedoes may have finished her off. She sank before dawn. The *Quincy*, which had been leading the parade, may have been hit in a magazine. Nonplussed witnesses of the disaster reported seeing bright flashes in the night in the direction of her approximate position. According to men on our Can there was another cruiser in the Tulagi patrol, but the Navy has not disclosed her name. She escaped. The *Quincy* sank.

The Japs, keeping their formation intact, headed out again on the Tulagi side. When the fighting commenced the destroyer on station on that side of Savo had anticipated some such maneuver and had run under the lee of the hummock-shaped island, prepared to let go her torpedoes as the Japs swept by. But she was challenged by another American destroyer, groping around in the darkness, which threw a searchlight on her. The Japs, making their getaway, spotted her then. Before she could get their range and bearing they had pulverized her thin steel hull with shells. Her compartments were flooded. She was obliged to jettison her torpedoes. She lay there, spiked and helpless, in her discovered ambush.

After the first assault our Can had put about to aid the *Canberra*. The Australian was flaming from stem to stern and settling. Captain Edmund Getting had given the order to abandon her and then had died of his wounds.

Our Can nosed in alongside of her despite the danger of explosions. Wounded men were lifted over the rail. Several, hurt and crippled, terrified by the licking fires, jumped and missed and plunged down between the two ships. Some eighty of the Australians had clambered or been lifted aboard our Can when officers watching the instruments on the bridge detected a ship approaching, hidden somewhere outside the area of light cast by the *Canberra's* flames. The order went out to stand by to engage. Men sprang back to their battle stations.

78

Through speaking trumpets officers on our Can shouted above the din to the *Canberra,* telling those who could to jump aboard, the rest of the wounded would have to be abandoned.

The Australians lined the rail of their stricken ship. They must have figured now they were surely doomed. But none of them jumped. The ablebodied chose to stay with the wounded. Lines were let go and our Can slid away. As she did the men aboard her heard a strange sound in that weird, noisy night.

"It was thrilling and heartbreaking," White told me. "The Australians were giving us three cheers."

Our Can sped in under the covering darkness. The approaching ship, with which she now had a good contact, might be a friend. In that moment of suspense and indecision someone switched on our Can's searchlight. The ghostly silhouette of a ship appeared, her gun muzzles suddenly marked by bright flashes. Our Can let go with her main battery. A shell from the other ship whistled just above our Can's bridge. But flare shells lighted the scene long enough for the ships to identify one another. Frantically the bridge gave the order to cease firing. The other vessel was the heavy cruiser *Chicago.*

The Navy has never revealed, if it knows, how many Jap ships were involved in the engagement. Congressman Melvin Maas, who was in the area as a Marine Corps reserve officer, asserted that the enemy had no more than three cruisers. If that was true it supported a theory held by many men on our Can— that some of the destruction that night was wreaked by our own ships, mixed up, milling around and firing at each other. The experience of the destroyer under the lee of Savo added circumstantial evidence to that theory. So did our Can's experience with the *Chicago.* In the words of one of the men it was "a bitched up show."

Our Can returned to the *Canberra.* Day was beginning to break. The *Vincennes* and *Quincy* were gone. The *Astoria,* little more than a carcass, was smoking and slowly sinking. The *Canberra* was put out of her misery with torpedoes. Aboard our Can Doc Moore and three doctors from the *Canberra* labored over the wounded who were packed into the wardroom, into officers' cabins, wherever a space could be found. Our

Can reeked with ether, disinfectant and blood. Some of the Australians died. Their mates tied blankets over their heads, lashed five-inch projectiles to their sides and buried them in the sea. Other casualties of the Battle of Savo Island perished with less dignity. In the grey and dismal dawn, the men of our Can recalled, the channel was dotted with curiously flopping, disembodied heads, shoulders and arms still upheld by Navy lifejackets. The waters off Savo Island, the men said, were swarming with sharks.

One of the mysteries of the night was the fate of the crippled *Jarvis*. She never made port. Careful search was made of the waters along the coast and of the shore itself. If the *Jarvis* had been destroyed by enemy action some wreckage would have floated. If she had foundered most of her crew would have been able to take to rafts. But not a stick of wreckage, not a raft, not a survivor was ever found. As far as searchers could ever report, no bodies were ever washed up on Guadalcanal's melancholy shores. The 1500-ton destroyer *Jarvis* simply vanished with all hands.

We raised the flowered island of Guadalcanal early the next morning and proceeded slowly along its shores. Along the warm water's edge were the coconut trees of the Lever Brothers' plantation. Beyond rose the 8000-foot-high jungle-clad mountain, the island's towering spine. Long grey tails of mist lay along the ridges, and the mountain's arched back was lost in its shroud of cottony clouds. It was only when you peered carefully through glasses that you saw the coconut groves had been torn by shot and the dark blotches along the beach were wrecked landing barges.

I asked White if I would be able to get ashore. He said he thought he could put me in somehow, though his ship would be underway all the time, screening the convoy while they unloaded. He could not guarantee that he would be within twenty or thirty miles of any given position at any time and I might even discover that he had gone off and left me. There was always the possibility of a sudden engagement. I decided to take a chance and borrowed a raincoat from one of the officers. It looked as though there was a squall making up over Tulagi.

X

THE BEACH

I WAS ANXIOUS TO GET ASHORE on Guadalcanal, if only for a
little while. The transport *John Penn* was anchored severed hundred yards offshore, while high-sided landing barges resembling
shoe boxes plied between the ship and the beach landing troops
and supplies. Our Can had to go to the *John Penn* to refuel and
her Executive Officer accommodatingly arranged a ride for me
in one of the barges. The squall broke as we were pulling away
from the ship. I sat on boxes of ammunition, unprotected from
the tropic deluge. The barge finally grated into the sand. I
climbed over the square bow and jumped out, water streaming
from the visor of a fishing cap I was wearing, soaked to my
skin despite the raincoat.

I was standing at last on the bloody and historical beach,
the dark and exotic island over which the United States and
Japan had fought for ten months. During that period virtually
all of the resources of the Pacific Fleet had been thrown into
the struggle to have and to hold the "Canal." Now it was ours.
But I probably have little sense of history, because I had no
particular awareness as I stood there except the awareness of
being wet.

Between the lapping waves and a grove of palm trees a narrow strip of sand was rutted by wheels and churned by feet. The
sand of Guadalcanal is black. A steel mat had been laid down
in one place and the barges rolled up to it, disgorging boxes,
sacks, tent poles and tents. Lines of drenched, bored-looking
men were engaged in toting these supplies up to slightly higher
ground and a clearing among the palm trees. The beachmaster,
a lieutenant from the *John Penn* in a sun helmet and a black
rubber coat, was directing the barge traffic, trying to keep the

line of toters moving and calling plaintively for more men all at the same time. But no one paid him any heed.

I plowed through the soft sand up to the clearing. A camp was being erected by a battalion of Marine Raiders. A few sagging khaki tents had been hoisted into place and gear, cots, blankets were piled underneath them. In one of the tents a major was sorting things out of the mud and gazing around his new home disconsolately. I stopped and introduced myself.

"You better come out of the rain," he invited.

I told him that I was really looking for Koli Point, since I understood that a Major Stewart of the Army was somewhere around there and someone had told me to look him up. My ideas of distances and locations on Guadalcanal were then pretty vague. His were too. He said he thought that Koli was several miles from this camp site. "And I don't know how you would get there," he said. "You can hardly get over the road in a jeep. They had a typhoon here two weeks ago that washed the roads out and wrecked all the bridges across the rivers and nobody's had time to fix the bridges since then."

"Well, I guess I'll look around here if you don't mind." The rain had stopped as suddenly as it had begun.

"Why sure—help yourself," said the major. "I'll look around with you. I haven't been any farther than this damn tent so far."

We waded through wet grass and mud, among palm trees and a debris of crushed coconuts and broken, emptied wooden boxes. Men were either standing around looking pained or were picking their way through the debris looking mysteriously troubled. "Isn't this a hell of a deal?" the major asked mildly.

On the edge of the jungle, which started on the other side of the clearing, stood a row of native grass huts, deserted and empty, and at the end of the row a larger building with a steep-thatched roof. It was also empty. By the faded symbols painted on the wooden cross-beams we judged it to be a church. It was as dry as a bone inside and I suggested, "Wouldn't this be a good place to store supplies?"

The major said yes but the orders were to respect the natives' property.

"How about the huts?"

82

"They're infested with bugs and mosquitoes."

The Marines were grimly resigned to their khaki tents and mud floors. There was no loud griping. The battalion recognized how much better things were than when the first Marines, less than a year ago, had settled on Guadalcanal. Instead of living on top of the mud those Marines had lived burrowed into it. They had starved in the mud and had been slain in the mud. We paused to gaze at an anomalous polished marble tombstone on the jungle's edge. Underneath it were the remains of a Catholic missionary. We went over to meet the major's colonel, who was also the regimental commander. The colonel was feeling somewhat encouraged. The cooks had got a bonfire going and were heating a big kettle of soup. The colonel considered it a triumph over nature. Rations so far had been cold. A captain and a lieutenant from a Construction Battalion nearby dropped in and asked in a neighborly way if they could be of any help. They had been on the island a week or so and were fairly well established. The colonel thanked them and said he would send an aide over if he needed anything.

I asked the two Seabees what they thought of my chances of getting to Koli Point. They thought the best thing was to hail a landing barge. The barges being used in the unloading were the *John Penn's* and would be tied up at that work, but there were barges from the Koli Point boat pool running along the shore all the time. They were going to walk back along the beach and suggested I go with them, maybe they could hail a ride for me. We plodded through the sand.

"There's one now," said the captain.

We all waved our arms and shouted. The craft was idling along some fifty yards out. Either the coxswain didn't hear us or he didn't want to; he never looked around. Instead he suddenly speeded up and was soon out of hailing distance. The captain and the lieutenant cursed. "That guy's going right down to Koli, too," the captain said. Barge coxswains, he informed me, were as independent as hogs on ice. "Bunch of damn young kids." We walked on, keeping our eyes out for another one.

Near the Seabee camp the tide had lifted a barge onto the beach and had left it there stranded high and dry. "Its engine quit," the lieutenant said bitterly, "so the crew just abandoned it and left it to float ashore. We've been trying to get it off. We're getting a bulldozer to see if we can move it."

The captain and I sat on a fallen palm tree and watched while the lieutenant went over and directed the salvage operations. A bulldozer had come clattering out of the jungle and it began to claw under the barge's bottom, the idea being to excavate to water so that the vessel could be floated. Another barge stood offshore, tugging at its sister with a steel cable.

Men moved listlessly. The only energetic feature in the picture was the bulldozer, which rushed around like a terrier rooting under a barn for mice, while the operator sweated and swayed and jounced up and down on his seat. The captain finally grunted, got up and went over to add his advice.

The sun was glaring down now and I sat steaming in my wet clothes too enervated by the heat to move. I had a drink from my canteen and speculated on the theories and problems of the Pacific campaign. Matériel, the Marine battalion and several hundred other troops being dumped ashore this morning by our convoy were obviously being moved up to take part in the forthcoming push. But that push was not coming off for a month or so. Meanwhile the troops in this spot would be more of a liability than an asset. Here they were four and a half days by water from the Noumea source of supply. Some of them would get malaria and dengue fever, cut themselves, shoot themselves, break their bones. They would get homesick and gloomy from inaction. The Japs would attack them periodically from the air. In this unhandy location they would have to be fed and cared for. Aircraft and ordnance would have to be expended to protect them. From time to time more troops and matériel would be dumped into raw jungles at the end of washed-out roads and the whole problem would mount like an arithmetical progression.

Clearly it would be better to move all the troops up in one big operation a few days before the push. But the catch was, the Navy did not have the ship bottoms for such an enterprise. The Navy only had a few merchantmen, transports, and tankers in this part of the world. The others were in the Atlantic. The overworked few had to shuttle back and forth, moving a few forces at a time up to the rim. Our offensives had to wait until we had accumulated enough strength on the rim. That was the chief reason for a creeping instead of a leaping advance in the Solomons.

The captain came back to announce that he saw a barge coming down from Koli and he thought that this one was going to land here. Sure enough, it did. The captain told the coxswain that I was coming aboard. I poised at the water's edge and when a wave receded leaped up onto the barge's high bow. These bows let down into convenient ramps but the coxswains can seldom be persuaded to go to all that trouble.

In the bright heat of the late morning we chugged along the coast to Koli. There was an ensign aboard from one of the small merchantmen which had come up in our convoy and he told me that his ship was practically unloaded. He said he thought they might be pulling out tonight. He said that cargo ships never stayed around Guadalcanal any longer than necessary because they never could tell when the Japs might show up. I began to feel a little anxious. Our Can might be detailed off to escort one of the first returning groups. I decided I had better get back aboard that afternoon.

Koli consisted of some finger piers, a signal tower built on stilts, and a few buildings along the beach. One of these was the headquarters for the boat pool. I inquired there if anyone had ever heard of Major W. S. Stewart but no one had. They thought that he might be down at Lunga Point. A jeep was starting for Lunga in a few minutes with the mail and I could go along if I wanted to. I asked the jeep driver when he would get back. "Sometime late this afternoon," he said. "It's about twelve miles but the roads are all shot to hell after the storm." I gave up the idea, asked him to mail a letter to Peg which I had brought with me, and walked across the road to a camp to beg some chow. It was noontime and I was hungry.

The camp belonged to one of the many land-based Navy units which were created especially for this island-to-island naval war. I went into the officers' mess and asked if they minded having a guest for lunch. It was the only way to get anything to eat.

The officers' mess was a bare wooden table with wooden benches seating about two dozen men. Lunch was hominy grits,

Harvard beets, cole slaw, water with a slightly lemony taste, bread and oleomargarine, and stewed apricots. There was also a bottle of yellow atabrine tablets which was passed around. Doc Moore had advised me to wait until I was on Guadalcanal to stay a while before I started the atabrine diet. The theory of atabrine was that if you had been bitten by the anopheles mosquito the atabrine would keep the fever suppressed only as long as you kept taking it. It was not a cure or a preventive. There was no point in taking it unless you thought you had run afoul of the anopheles.

Among the officers at the table was a young man who introduced himself as J. L. Lord, of Orange, New Jersey, who once had also been a commuter to New York on the D.L.&W. He had worked for the Guaranty Trust. The boss of the unit was Commander Harris Carrigan of San Francisco, who was well acquainted, it turned out, with Dave Hulburd, the ubiquitous head of our News Bureau.

Carrigan invited me to inspect his camp site when I had finished lunch. He was still in the process of getting settled but he had been there longer than the Marines and was fairly well fixed. He had foxholes, drainage ditches, and electric lights. Under a tarpaulin was a treasure trove of washing machines—half a dozen of them. And in a tent known as the recreation tent was a small piano which had been donated by a lady in San Francisco, which needed a little tinkering with but was going to be all right.

Such luxuries as this were certainly not consistent with the stories I had read of the island. Carrigan said the place had lately grown quite civilized. New arrivals like the Marine Raiders who had to start housekeeping in undeveloped sites had a rugged time of it, he said. But in some of the older communities like Lunga Point and Henderson Field there were all kinds of comforts.

Carrigan led me along a grassy path to his tent. It had nothing to distinguish it as the commander's. Camp sites are not laid out in parade ground fashion any more. They are spread haphazardly around the terrain. The idea is to make them inconspicuous rather than precise. We sat on a box in Carrigan's tent.

He exhibited a collection of mosquito bites on his legs. "Since we got these lights run in," he explained, "I sit up nights read· ing. You should get under a mosquito net as soon as it's dark. But I haven't gotten malaria yet." He reached over and knocked on the wooden tent pole, from which a single unshaded light bulb was suspended. He asked me if I would like a drink of gin and brought out a bottle of gin and a bottle of Angostura Bitters. "Gin and bitters for the tropics," he said and dashed some Angostura into a shot of warm gin which I diluted with some warm water from my canteen. I felt quite cheered up.

Carrigan said he had all kinds of men in his unit—ordinary laborers, artisans, businessmen, doctors, lawyers. "That fellow over there," he said pointing under the tent flap, "was once a fashionable undertaker in Kansas City. I asked him what he could do and he said, 'I'm used to handling men,' so I made him my personnel officer."

The ex-undertaker came to the tent to ask Carrigan a question then and Carrigan told me he would have to go and earn his salary but he hoped I would drop in again. Would I give his love to his sister in San Francisco if I went through there on my way home? I said I would.

I wandered through the camp. J. L. Lord and a lieutenant were gazing at a big, dirty, khaki-colored truck which had just come out of the jungle. Painted on its side in big yellow letters was DOTTY. "Some of these kids get hold of a little paint and they go hog-wild," the lieutenant told me morosely. "You've got to keep the paint under lock and key." Dotty was the name of the lieutenant's girl.

The sun was beginning to slant through the towering jungles. I went back to boat pool headquarters and asked if there were any barges going out to ships. They told me to ask the Director of the Port, who was sitting on the pier. A yeoman offered to point him out and took me across the road where a man in a sun helmet was sitting with his head between his knees. "Here's a war correspondent wants to get aboard a ship," said the yeoman. The Director of the Port, a lieutenant, shuddered, lifted his head and gave me the stare of a man who is resigned to almost anything but this.

"Any ship, it doesn't matter," I said.

A barge was just pulling out. He got up and called to the coxswain to wait a minute. As I jumped aboard he shouted after me, "I just got word that about a dozen of you guys are on their way up here."

There wasn't time to ask him for details. We were heading out into the straits and it began almost immediately to rain in another one of those violent tropic downpours. Most of the crowd I had left at Noumea must be moving up, if what the Port Director said was true. There was a possibility that the date for the push had been advanced but I doubted it. I had an impulse to stay on the island, but in the end decided to stay aboard the Can and return to Noumea. I could always get back in a hurry by plane, I thought.

I told the coxswain the number of our Can and he pointed to a ship moving along through the rain off our starboard bow. "I think that's her," he said. "If it is I can intercept her. If it ain't you're out of luck. I'll have to stick you aboard another ship. I can't go looking all over for your ship." I was glad to see after a moment that it was. The crew of the barge semaphored our Can and someone on the bridge semaphored back. Our Can slowed down and we ran under her lee. With the barge bucking under me, soaked by rain and spray, I grabbed a rope ladder, climbed up and over the rail and landed on deck. Lieutenant (jg) Chappel Foote was there to set me upright.

Red was in the cabin sound asleep on his nice dry comfortable bunk. I got my wet clothes off and padded down to the two-stall shower in the officers' head, bathed in hot water and dried myself on a big rough Navy towel, musing over the comforts of life at sea as compared to life on a tropic island.

That night in the wardroom I described the lot of the Marine Raiders and the lunch of hominy grits at Carrigan's camp while we ate steak and Madison's lemon meringue pie. A soldier's life was a pretty bum deal, they agreed smugly.

But I have heard the other point of view from soldiers. A sergeant told me, "Sure it's nice life on a ship if you don't get seasick and so on. But when the shooting starts I like to have a lot of ground under my feet in case I want to go somewheres else. The trouble with a ship, mister, is you can't get off it and get the hell out of there. You got to stay and take it. By and large, mister, when there's a war on I prefer the infantry."

One man's meat is another's poison. Commander Glynn Robert Donaho, captain of a submarine, vowed that his was the best service. "Absolutely the safest," he said. "All you have to do when you're under attack is submerge."

XI

SUBMARINE CONTACT

Our can was not sent back with the first ships after all. We patrolled the straits for another day and a half and finally headed south with just one ship, the slab-sided *John Penn*. There had been no sign or report of the enemy and I for one relaxed. It seemed to me unlikely that the Japs would bother with one transport homeward bound, riding high, obviously empty. It was always more worthwhile to sink a laden ship.

The wardroom, however, did not share my complacency. One warship is meagre protection, even for one ship, they pointed out. It is almost impossible for a single vessel guarding another to watch all quarters from which the enemy can attack. The men on our Can recalled an occasion off the Australian coast when they were convoying a lone freighter. It was a bright and peaceful afternoon with no suspicion of the enemy's presence. But a lookout suddenly noticed that the freighter had stopped. In a matter of seconds she had vanished. Survivors reported that she had taken a torpedo which had broken her back. She had been picked off by an ambushing submarine which our Can had easily missed in the wide area which she had to cover.

It was also easy for a submarine to draw off a single escort while a second sub went in and killed the helpless merchantman.

But I began to enjoy the trip home, lolling on the signal flag box, acquiring a good tan to go with my war correspondent's costume. There were several days of vigorous bucking and rolling in a heavy sea when I felt a little squeamish, but I attended all meals and even grew fat on Madison's pastries. One of the two ensigns who had been seasick all the way north had recovered his equanimity while we were patrolling the quiet straits.

90

He had decided that he had licked seasickness and that he was going to be all right from then on. But we had hardly stuck our nose into the Coral Sea again when his misery returned. I remember him standing his bridge watch, wan and drawn and silent again, while his colleagues loudly discussed such favorite dishes as fried pork chops and onions. For him destroyer life had no good features. The other ensign had been transferred to another can. I don't know how he made out.

White liked to quote someone who said that war was 90 per cent sheer boredom and 10 per cent sheer terror. I was even getting bored.

I was sitting in the cabin one night writing a letter. The Can was pitching violently. Every once in a while the chair took a trip across the room with me on it wildly grabbing for a handhold. In one of her letters Peg had asked for some advice about the girls' studies. They had to make out next year's school programs. I felt remote from the problem, here in the middle of the Coral Sea, so I hedged: "I thought Nancy and I figured out pretty well what her schedule would be for the next three years. I agree with you that the twins ought to take some Latin before they take French." I got around to more familiar subjects: "We've seen a lot of flying fish," I wrote. "The doctor told me that he once picked up some which had been washed aboard, had them cooked and ate them for breakfast. He said they were very tasty...." At about this point in my letter the alarm squawked.

My first thought was, It's some kind of a test. But almost immediately Doc Moore came out of the cabin which he shared with "Pay" Whitaker and I heard him say: "That's a submarine contact." I pulled the curtain back and saw Doc standing there with his tin helmet on and tying the strings of his lifejacket. I screwed on the cap of my pen and stood up. I felt solemn. I put on my helmet and kapok jacket. Doc had gone on out and several other officers had already hurried along the passageway.

A kind of electric charge passes through a ship when something goes amiss. You can sense the difference in men's footsteps along the steel decks. Ordinary conversations suddenly cease and there is a new sharpness in voices. I went out to the passageway and at that moment the alarm began to squawk repetitively, *waah, waah, waah*—General Quarters!

I spun the big wheel on the door that opened onto the weather deck. As the bolts slid back the red light in the passageway automatically went out. I stepped over the high sill. It was necessary to brace yourself on the rolling deck while you spun the wheel on the outside to secure the door again. The deck was little more than a platform, one stage in the ascent to the navigating bridge. I never did get accustomed to stepping from lighted quarters into the pitchblack darkness of a weather deck. It was a strange, wet, pitching world through which you groped in your night blindness. Just then there came a muffled, jarring concussion.

I found and hung onto the rail. I thought that we must have been torpedoed. I could feel the whole ship shuddering under the impact of the explosion. I had no idea what to do next. If the ship went down, what chance was there of being picked up in this black void of ocean? I could hear nothing but the deep swish of water along our side. I tried to picture myself floating in the sea in a lifejacket and leaned over the rail. I could see the vague white streak of our wake. It occurred to me that we couldn't have been torpedoed or we would have lost way. There was a sudden flicker of dull light which I realized was heat lightning on the far horizon. I decided to go up to the bridge. I had a queer feeling in my throat. I was feeling along the rail to the companionway when I heard the rattle of the door being opened and secured again. People brushed past me, though I couldn't see them. No one spoke. I heard their feet going *bang, bang* up the inclined ladder and I finally found the handrail and ran up after them. There was another small deck where I had to feel my way around stanchions. I located the last ladder, gained the bridge.

It was crowded with officers, chiefs, signalmen, talkers. In the dark confusion of the wheelhouse there were no lights but the faint ones on the dials. Red Quigley, hunched over his chart table, held a tiny red flashlight which he carefully shielded as he worked on a chart, tracing our shifting course. I gradually figured out what was happening. We had a submarine contact

92

and were running it down, trying to get into position to depth charge it.

A depth charge, I guessed, was what had caused the concussion. I found out later that this was correct. Our sonic devices had picked up the whir of torpedo screws. Somewhere in the cavernous night a sub had detected either us or the *John Penn* and had launched a fish. We had promptly dropped an "embarrassing charge," which is an ashcan put over in the faint hope of (1) exploding the onrushing torpedo, (2) making the sub think that she has scored a hit.

There was a confusion of noises, the chirp of the sound detector, a babel of voices. I tried to sort the voices out. Part of the babel was Al White talking over the between-ships radio to the skipper of the *John Penn,* advising him of our intentions, and the Penn's skipper answering back. There were voices giving the bearing and range of the contact. There were orders to increase speed, slow down, increase again as we stalked our prey —orders to the helmsman, orders repeated back, orders relayed by talkers.

Voices grew hard and edgy. Over the talker system Lieutenant Jim Foote asked the sound detector room if they still had the contact. There was no answer. Twice more Foote repeated the question, his voice getting louder and louder: "Do you still have a contact—yes or no?"

"No, sir," a voice finally said.

Someone swore with vexation: "For Christ's sake!" The sub had escaped us then. I was feeling a lot more confidence now, surrounded by my fellow men. I had begun to appreciate the capabilities of our destroyer and I was infected with the excitement of the chase. I would liked to have gone back to Noumea and reported that we had killed a Jap sub. I was vexed too.

Then, in another of those dull lightning flashes on the horizon we saw, or thought we saw, a ship's silhouette. A voice began to crackle over our talker system. The blackness closed around us again. I thought this second vessel might be another submarine, surfaced. We changed course, heading for where it had been.

I remembered what they had told me about one submarine drawing the escort ship off while a second closed on the convoy.

I supposed we would not get too far from the defenseless *John Penn*. We were at full speed, racing through the starless night. In a moment of abrupt silence in the wheelhouse a man on the platform above must have dropped a tool because something clanged loudly on the overhead.

These fellows knew the sudden and catastrophic possibilities of a nighttime naval engagement. We had no idea what kind of hostile forces were gathering around us in the night. I had the queer feeling again in my throat.

The guns in our Number 1 and Number 2 turrets were trained. We could open up, then illuminate the target with star shells.

But it might be a friendly ship. That was the hazard of opening fire before we had identified her beyond any question of doubt. The hazard of holding our fire was that it gave the enemy a chance to get in the first salvo, always a terrible advantage. We were rapidly closing in. Men scowled into the darkness through night glasses.

"Range four-eight-oh-oh. . . . Range three-five-oh-oh. . . ."

White suddenly said: "Challenge."

The shutter on a blinker light went tat-a-tat-a-tat-tat. A signalman was flashing the code challenge which any friendly ship would recognize. Our position was revealed. We were like people waiting for an explosion—tense, holding our breaths. In the captain's mind, I suppose, was some kind of stopwatch counting off the fractions of seconds before he gave the order to fire. *One, two, three*—then it flickered, a frantic, frightened blinking in the night.

She identified herself as a flush-deck destroyer, headed north with another Allied convoy.

The bridge relaxed. I drew a deep breath. In a high, thin voice a boy said, "If that guy knew how close he came to getting it. . . . What the hell was he waiting for? Why didn't he identify himself before?"

White gave the order to change course and the helmsman repeated the order. The helmsman was one of the older CPO's and he made it a point to sound very casual and matter-of-fact. Over the radio came the voice of the *John Penn*'s skipper: "Joe from Dick—I feel kind of naked out here." White told him that we were hastening to return.

Instead of pitching, we began to roll. Broadside to the sea now, we sashayed back to our station. We took up our endless zigzagging and search, beating our way south again for Noumea. We secured from General Quarters and the bridge returned to its normal complement of men on watch. I went down to the wardroom for a cup of coffee and listened to a description of our maneuvers. I finally went back to the cabin and finished my letter. "I am well and having an interesting time, etc., etc."

It was the only excitement.

We delivered the *Penn*. On a dirty, rainy afternoon we threaded our way back up the tortuous channel and into the harbor, where the warships sat majestically at anchor. That night the captain left the bridge for the first time in two weeks, flopped on the bunk in his cabin next to ours and went to sleep. Blinkers gossiped about us from the summits of the overhanging hills and from sister ships moored around us. The mail came aboard—sugar reports from Sydney and from back home. From the Port Director came instructions to send a work party ashore the first thing in the morning to pick up the new detector equipment. It had been shipped out from America and would be installed here. That was that. Our Can could not be spared long enough to go back to the West Coast for a Navy Yard job. It would be some time yet before Red saw his strawberry blonde. In the wardroom the officers produced a coffee can full of Australian coins, which, they told me, they used for chips. They found out that this war correspondent was easy poker meat.

In the morning we moved to a place alongside a tender. All hands turned to, hammering, chipping, painting. My cabin was filled with the din. I ventured out on deck. On the platform above the bridge a man was working with an acetylene torch and sparks rained down on me. "You never get any damn peace when you're in port," White said. I had told him the night before that I was going to leave him in the morning. Now he said good-bye. He sent me ashore in his launch.

There was no peace and little surcease any time for the Navy's destroyers, I decided. In the launch I chugged past the haughty warships waiting for something important to send them to sea.

XII

ADVANCE BASE

Home to a war correspondent is where he gets his mail and parks his dirty clothes. I therefore went directly to the Quonset hut which housed the Navy PRO. Particularly I wanted to find out what was happening up north that required the arrival in Guadalcanal of a dozen newspaper reporters. Four or five correspondents were sitting around the hut when I arrived. They scarcely looked up at the voyager returning from a hazardous convoy, but one of them finally asked casually if I had had a good trip. I was a little taken aback but I said just as casually: "All right—no action."

It was true that most of the crowd had gone. Bill Shrout had gone, Wolfert had gone. Tom Lambert had put all this journalistic talent aboard one transport. At Guadalcanal they would all be attached to Com-Amphib-For-So-Pac—the cryptic designation for Commander of Amphibious Forces in the South Pacific.

I assumed the proper air of offhand interest. When is the show coming off? June 30. Do we know anything about the plans? The plans are to seize the enemy base at Munda on the island of New Georgia, 180 miles north of Henderson Field. The Solomons attack will be synchronized with an offensive which MacArthur is going to launch in his area, the idea being to give the Jap no chance to concentrate his defense in one spot. If successful it could be the first major Allied offensive on the South Pacific front since the landing on Guadalcanal in August, 1942.

I conferred with Tom over the best way to see it. All the places assigned to the press with the main amphibious forces had been allotted to the correspondents who had departed and they had hurried off because they wanted to nail down their positions. As far as that deal was concerned I was a Johnny-come-lately. I felt that I had been euchred out of a place, although it was probably my own fault. I had not been on hand to make any claim. Anyhow, Tom said comfortingly, there were a number of other deals, to wit:

I could accompany one of several Raider battalions going ashore at points on the southern end of New Georgia—Munda was in the north. These landings would probably be resisted and might turn out to be interesting. I could go aboard one of the destroyers which would escort the landing ships into the harbor. Or I could be accredited to Rear Admiral Mark Mitscher's Com-Air-Sol, which would direct air operations from Guadalcanal, where Allied air forces were based. Admiral Mitscher would get first reports of the battle and I would be able to watch some of the show from observation planes.

I considered. I was prejudiced against flying in combat areas, and I had promised myself that I would not go on any air combat missions. That kind of story had been done so often that it was no longer a novelty. The results, I thought, were scarcely ever worth the hazards and correspondents who ran the risk were simple-minded and reckless. But if I could go on more or less safe observation missions—especially with a high-ranking official along to insure against the taking of any unreasonable risks—I would probably enjoy the experience. From the air an amphibious invasion must be a spectacular sight. So I asked Tom to accredit me to Com-Air-Sol and get me transported back to Guadalcanal.

This is the uncertain way in which correspondents of necessity cover wars. They choose their spot and hope that the action will flow in their direction. In my case I hoped that not too much action would flow in my direction.

Tom said that it would be several days before I could get away again. There were no convoys due to leave very soon. The one on which the others had departed—and which must have been the one we had encountered on the way home—had been a sizable force and it would be some little time before another was loaded and ready to move. Air transportation to Guadalcanal was momentarily out of the question. Transport planes

97

had been grounded for the last several days by bad weather and a lot of high priority passengers were waiting in line. But I need not worry about missing the show. Tom would get me there, he promised. Meanwhile I could move into the village of Quonset huts which housed the headquarters staff. There was a hut there for correspondents and I could sleep between sheets which had covered some well-known newspapermen.

I was grateful. I had already discovered that the fretful business of finding a place to sleep and eat, getting clothes washed, replenishing supplies, getting oneself bathed and shaved frequently took hours of arranging and maneuvering. I had been able to have laundry done aboard the destroyer but an immediate problem was the bag of dirty clothes which I had left at the hut. In the PRO jeep Leif Erickson drove me around to a tumbledown house near the Hotel Pacifique. There lived a laundress whom he had discovered after much searching. She was a little, button-eyed native, married to a Frenchman, and she obligingly agreed to have my laundry done on whatever day I said—*lundi, mardi, mercredi*—although the day I actually got it, Leif said, would be something else. Still, her price was reasonable and the washing came back clean. Such trivial business took time. I suppose a good deal of time is expended on these things at home but I had never been aware of it. My drawer was always full of freshly laundered shirts and I did not inquire into the matter.

It made me impatient to have to expend so much of the day on these routines. I lost a razor, for example, during one of my trips at sea. I had come by this razor easily enough. I had simply expressed a desire for one of this particular brand and on my birthday there it was, neatly wrapped and lovingly labelled: "To Daddy." I was sorry to lose it but certainly never anticipated that I would have to consume the better part of two days in Noumea getting another. Razors, I found out while I was borrowing one from Joe Driscoll, were practically unobtainable in New Caledonia. I drove miles in the jeep trying PX's at various camps in the hill and along the shore. I tried native shops in town. I considered following the example of Cant of the *Post*. On that last night at the Halekulani when Cant had popped in from New York he had been wearing a neat little

98

moustache. He popped into Noumea wearing a handsome beard. The unexpected way I finally came on a razor was simply a piece of luck.

I had decided to try, as a last resort, a Navy small stores on the waterfront. I stood in line for almost an hour, shooting the breeze with a New Zealand soldier in front of me and watching a sombre French funeral drag by—only to get to the window and have the clerk tell me: "No razors." But as I was backing away he gave me a darting look, leaned forward and said in a low voice which the man behind me was not supposed to hear: "Look, I've got one back at my camp. I'll bring it in tomorrow morning. You be here and I'll have it for you. O.K.?"

"O.K.," I said. "Will you be at this window—or who shall I ask for?" He jerked his head. "Go around to the side door and ask for Joe."

I was there the next morning and stealthily asked for Joe. He came out with a razor in a box and a package of blades. "I'll bet you thought I wouldn't bring it," he said. I lied, "No—I was sure you would. How much do I owe you?" I was prepared, of course, to pay through the nose, caught as I thought I was in a very black market.

"Aw, hell," he said. "Nothin'. What would I do with the money in this dump? I just happened to have an extra one. It's yours."

The wonder to me, though, was not the scarcity of some items but the fact that there was so much familiar American merchandise to be had—such things as Palmolive soap, Parker's Quink. I thought it was typical of American genius that in the midst of shipping howitzers and tanks someone had thought to include Quink.

The whole big base at Noumea was an example of American genius for thinking of things. When France collapsed in 1940 Noumea was a threadbare, cockroach-ridden colonial port run by a Vichy governor, defended by a few garrison troops, with some ancient cannon pointing across its fine harbor. Population was around 12,000, consisted of French, half castes (the French actively intermarry), mixed native Polynesians and Melanesians, Tonkinese and Javanese. The town's chief enterprise was the nickel smelter on the waterfront, an ancient and outmoded plant which depended extensively on the slow hand labor of the Tonkinese and Javanese who had been imported for it. The easygoing natives declined to be sucked into this industrial vortex.

The French got rid of their Vichy governor—though not their cockroaches—on September 19, 1940, and in the spring of 1942 war and the U. S. Navy moved in on neglected Noumea. By the time I arrived there it had become the keypoint of our South Pacific campaign, a place to hold and deny the enemy, a vital link in our line to Australia, and a great repository of men and matériel.

Rear Admiral Robert Ghormley, whose edict on neckties had caused me some concern in Pearl Harbor, had begun the swift development of the place in the summer of 1942. Some of the history of the undertaking was told to me by the Director of the Port, whose name Navy censorship in Pearl Harbor would not let me reveal; why I am at a loss to say. There were other details which the Navy declined to let me reveal for the very good reason that they might tell the enemy more about our methods of operation than it was good for him to know.

"Tank farms" (fuel storage tanks) were established around the mountainous coastline. An organization to run the port was set up and installed ashore.

There was little to build from when the work of creating this military establishment began. The broken-down utilities of the slovenly little town were scarcely adequate for its own needs. Sanitation was primitive. The rest of the cigar-shaped island was wild, undeveloped, threaded by rushing mountain streams. In the whole of 250-mile-long New Caledonia dwelt hardly more than 50,000 people. Seabees and other Navy construction units had to pioneer in the mountains among the *niaouli* groves before they could actually get to work on the building of roads, reservoirs, fuel and ammunition dumps, warehouses, repair shops, barracks and hospitals.

Ships from Australia, New Zealand, the United States hauled timber for dockpiles, strip steel for Quonset huts, steel plates for pontoons, pipes for plumbing, men and machinery to do the digging and erecting and assembling, and overnight a town of thousands of men whose business was war was superimposed

100

upon a town of a few thousand outnumbered, bewildered colonials. As installations mushroomed the Navy put its administration and maintenance crews ashore.

These were the units to one of which my friend Carrigan in Guadalcanal belonged. It is the Navy's army, in a manner of speaking, a creation unique in the history of naval warfare, conceived to fit the peculiar needs of a Pacific campaign which has to be fought over thousands of miles of sea from dozens of nondescript little ocean islands. The men of this new branch of the U.S. Navy have nothing whatever to do with the sailing of ships. They receive no training for sea duty and only a modicum of combat training of any kind. They are construction men—like the Seabees—administrators, engineers, specialists in communication and detection systems, instructors, medical men, lawyers, recreational directors—sailors with mud on their shoes who brought from their civilian jobs the talent and experience the Navy needed.

The Director of the Port, a large, bearlike kind of man, related in an aside how the war effort was threatened one morning by a swarm of bees which invaded his office. Among his versatile personnel, the alarmed Director learned, was an amateur apiarist who fortunately had brought along all his paraphernalia and quickly saved Noumea.

Each of these special units performs its special chore. One maintains airports. Others service various types of aircraft. Another is a shore unit with functions roughly equivalent to a floating tender. Others direct harbor traffic, arrange pilotage facilities, anchorages and operate harbor boats. One unit assembles the boxlike pontoons which are bolted together in rows or blocks as the occasion demands and used as docks, bridges, lighters—with engines mounted on them, as self-propelled barges. Others police the streets, run the utilities. Others operate barbecues and beer gardens for shoregoing gobs. Others conduct schools for the further instruction of officers and men. One organization distributes the movie shows which every night noisily unspin on the ships in the winking harbor, on the bare starlit hillsides and in the dark alleyways of tent cities. New Zealanders and British sailors think this is the typical last touch. No doubt it is. No war has ever been conducted with so much high-class entertainment.

The Director of the Port naturally would not tell me the size of this land Navy. But he did say that in the immediate area of the base were more men than there were in the whole U.S. Navy in 1939 and 30 per cent of them were stationed on shore. This was vague, as it was intended to be. But it conveyed some idea of the importance in the Pacific war of the sailors who never go near the water.

New Caledonia was an over-sized working model, the Director said, of the bases which the Navy was prepared to build right across the Pacific. He said the New Caledonia base was not completed, probably never would be. One admiral had declared: "It is our intention to leave half finished bases all the way to Tokyo."

Neither the Director, who had spent most of his career at sea, nor any other Navy officer I talked to in Noumea cared to predict what would happen to New Caledonia after the war. Certainly if we intend to dominate the Pacific we will have to continue to occupy the island. Aside from its importance to us as a base, New Caledonia will be then, as it is now, a place to deny the enemy. Beyond its deep, now heavily fortified harbor, lie mountains filled with minerals: nickel and chromite which are being shipped to American war plants; cobalt and iron. But we have no title. France will probably want back her once neglected stepchild.

XIII

THE THIN LINE

THE POPULATION OF NOUMEA reacted uncertainly at first to the peaceful but overwhelming invasion. There were the usual crises. One French farmer with a beautiful daughter was said to have asked that an armed guard be posted at his gate. Another Frenchman was said to have publicly announced that one of his two beautiful daughters was a leper; he did not say which one. But the Americans were well behaved—at any rate as well behaved as they are at home. There were expected crises over property, to which Navy attorneys attended. Overlapping official functions of the government and the military were adjusted and life resumed much as usual, except that a few local businesses—laundry, picture postcards, soft drinks—boomed.

Preoccupied with the military aspect of the town I found too little time to investigate the town itself. But in a book store I encountered a courtly gentleman who introduced himself as Sidney Reichenbach and the author of a pamphlet entitled *All you want to know about New Caledonia—Illustrated Edition*. I bought M. Reichenbach's book, which he signed with his compliments, and learned a number of things about the island which America has borrowed, and where thousands of Americans have been dumped.

The climate is "reputedly very healthy," M. Reichenbach reports. He told me that he had lived there all his life and he looked hale and hearty when I ran into him in *la boutique*. I do not know why he was so cautious about it in his report.

The hottest days are in December, January, and February, when temperatures run from 77 to 86 in the shade, Mr. Reichenbach goes on. This is also the season when cyclones swoop.

The cool season begins in May, when mountain temperatures sometimes drop to 45.

The native Melanesians, with whom the Polynesians have been richly mixed, were "still at the stone age" no less than 100 years ago. And because animals did not exist on the island until white men imported them *"of course* (the natives) were cannibals"—an explanation of cannibalism which I never before appreciated, though it may be generally recognized. I never though much about cannibalism except in a distant way.

The natives are now Christianized though they have accepted the faith with, M. Reichenbach feels, their tongues in their cheeks. They have their reliable wooden gods handy, respect their tribal sorcerer next to their tribal chief, and keep a watchful eye over their shoulder for the devils that roam in the bush.

Captain Cook discovered the island in 1774, at the sight of its mountainous profile thought nostalgically of Scotland, and so christened it.

France took possession of New Caledonia in 1853 and ten years later made it a convict settlement, moving 15,000 case-hardened criminals to its shores along with 3500 political deportees, who were, many of them, "men of superior intellect and standing." France gave up the practice in 1895. After that two attempts were made to settle the island with free Frenchmen but neither attempt was very successful.

The chief industries in the order of their importance are: mining, coffee planting, cattle raising.

Smaller industries are: troca-shell fishing, copra gathering, manufacture of *essence di niaouli* (used in medicines for colds), growing of sugar cane. New Caledonia once manufactured a "perfect rhum" called *Rhum Bacouya.* The business was abandoned because, like many of the island's enterprises, "except for the local trade no outlet existed." M. Reichenbach charges: "Australia, though supplying to us almost as much goods as did France, bought from us absolutely nothing."

The back country swarms with wild deer, wild dogs, wild pigs, wild ducks and the *notou,* a pigeon. Snakes are non-existent.

Tourist traffic has been spasmodic in the past. A Vanderbilt yacht called at the island four years ago.

The reef-sheltered seas around are a fisherman's heaven. "It is commonplace to catch 20 different types of fish in one day's outing."

104

The population supports the Allied cause. M. Reichenbach describes the revolution against a Vichy-sympathizing Governor Pelissier, which was a people's revolt. A bomb was tossed into Government House gardens "as a warning" to Pelissier to abdictate. He got out fast, fleeing *en famille* by air, leaving a Colonel Denis behind to do what he could. "Our present and very much esteemed Governor Sautot," M. Reichenbach writes, "landed on the now historic date of 19th September 1940, at the Noumean wharf only a few yards away from a French man-o'-war whose officers had Vichy sentiments and whose Commander had repeatedly threatened the Noumean population with bombardment. The landing was effected about noon under the delirious acclamations and joy of the people."

Broussards, the men of the back country, armed with hunting rifles, poured in from the hills to reinforce the townspeople. Denis was taken prisoner without bloodshed and the day was won for Free France.

Closer-up, Noumea was disappointing. It frequently stunk of its open sewers. It was soiled and cracked—a badly painted, faded backdrop in this little sidestreet theatre of the war. Board and stucco buildings, shuttered and blank, butted up against the dirt sidewalks. Shops were dark and dusty, merchandise was scattered around on half-empty shelves. The best looked like the poorest American country stores. Weeds grew over the fences in the yards of frowsy bungalows. In the middle of an unkempt park a Hero reared on his pedestal but his legend was dimmed by weather and neglect.

Against the backdrop moved the population. Elderly, pale colonials in choke-collar linen coats stumped along the streets or steered their bony wives cautiously around in tinny French cars. Women in long out-of-fashion dresses filed solemnly up to the cathedral on the hill. Little girls with long ribbons dangling from broad-brimmed hats which little American girls called Madge Evans hats in 1916, long-legged little boys with elderly faces and skin-tight shorts skittered like flocks of chickens back and forth to school. Tiny, willowy Javanese women in ankle-length sarongs padded along the paths on bare, flat feet. Black, big-bottomed Melanesian women swayed past grinning and gobbling. Muscular Melanesian men dressed in shorts and gym shirts ambled lazily through the mud, their bullpup faces and fuzzy, orange-stained hair giving them a formidable air mitigated somewhat by the flowers stuck behind their ears, the necklaces of beer bottle tops around their necks.

Occasionally the population paused to stare at the khaki trucks that squeezed and thundered through the narrow streets, or trailers hauling torpedoes, or field pieces jouncing by, or jeeps and station wagons filled with admirals and captains and commanders and lieutenants commuting back and forth from the naval suburbs in the hills to offices in town. But the population had no lines to speak. They were merely walk-on characters in the show.

The camp where I spent the next few days was a typical naval suburb. It was exclusively for staff officers and exclusively Quonset huts. These huts, slapped together out of half-circle sections of strip steel, were very practical indeed. They could be made indefinite lengths by simply adding more sections. They had a small porch at either end, screened-in doors and windows and were cool and comfortable. They were fairly weather-tight, insulated against the heat by wallboard, and tethered to the ground by wire nets in case of cyclones. The only buildings in our camp which were not Quonset huts were the little square-sided privies and the washrooms; these were tailor-made and wooden.

Our colony was built on the side of a hill. At the top were the mess hall with the galley next door and the wine mess with a bar at one end where officers who had paid a deposit could order and usually get Scotch, bourbon, rye, rum, gin, beer and sign a chit. The wine mess opened onto a terrace which overlooked a pretty estuary of Noumea Harbor. Downward led a coral-pebble path which eased past the open-air movie theatre, officers' huts and finally came to the correspondents' hut and that was all; that was the end.

Our hut, as I remember it, had sagging beds for eight men. Some of the officers' huts had fewer, and consequently more room for odds and ends of furniture. We each had a bedside table and a plywood locker the size of a coffin set on end, and there we could store clothes, gear, beer. Ours was not the neatest hut in the village. Because most of us were transients

106

I suppose we did not have the same pride as the other tenants. We were happy so long as the orderly carted away the beer cans in the mornings before they attracted too many flies.

Aside from the arguing that went on among the men in our hut, whom Jack Mahon referred to as the "little chicos," the village had an almost perpetual Sunday morning quiet. By eight o'clock in the morning the officers had herded themselves into cars and were joggling down their breakfasts on their way past the old French fort and the fez-topped sentry on guard to the long hill into town. In the evenings they got back in time to sit on the terrace, nibble salted peanuts, sip highballs and play poker dice for drinks before mess. Afterwards they went to the movies, either at our camp or one nearby, played poker, read and went to bed.

It was a bachelor life—comfortable except for cold-water shaves and showers; casual; free of female fury.

Some of the men at our camp had seen action and had been hospitalized back and given this station. Some of them never had and never would see action. While wives worried over "him" in the Pacific he was as safe as though he had been at home. His greatest hazards were dysentery and getting run over by a jeep and these hazards were slight because he almost never walked, drank chlorinated water and ate carefully inspected American food prepared by Navy cooks.

But he was not happy. Here was White's 90 per cent of utter boredom. The more I saw of the war the more I realized how, over the months, most of the time is spent by men waiting, or men working at this kind of dull and peaceful assignment. Their endless, tiresome duty gets no reporting because there is nothing dramatic to report. Obviously the jobs are necessary. Behind every spasmodic burst of energy, which in seconds may end in the destruction of an enemy ship, the capture of a beachhead, the annihilation of a bomber squadron go the hours of staff-work, administering, organizing, paper-shuffling.

That was the way in which the staff officers in our community tried to reconcile themselves. They tried halfheartedly to interrupt the boredom. One officer dug and cultivated a little garden plot. Occasionally they held a dance in the mess hall and hopefully invited the formidable Wacs, civilian workers, and Navy

107

nurses who were stationed around Noumea. Afterwards they sat around gazing glumly at Varga pin-ups, deciding that nature had double-crossed them. The morning after they got back in the station wagons with slight headaches as usual. At noon they came back to lunch. In the evening they returned as usual to sit on the terrace until chowtime, watching one of Noumea's overdone sunsets. Over the door of one hut was a large sign which read "Societe de P——d-Off Patriots."

It was time, finally, to move. Tom had transportation for Allan Jackson, of International News Photos, and me aboard the *John Penn*. We chugged out into the harbor in one of the Navy's big motor launches. These embarkations were never the effortless procedure they sound like. Passengers had to get their own baggage aboard. I carried dangling over my shoulder a musette bag into which I had stuffed a canteen and a mosquito netting, with my tin helmet strapped on the outside and a GI raincoat slung through the straps. That gave me two almost free hands to drag, heave and bully a kit bag of close to sixty deadweight pounds. Oftener the kit bag bullied me. I am a small man and I weigh not much more than twice what the bag did. The job of covering a war never looked so monumental as it did when I stood in a small boat, encumbered with all this gear, and gazed up the towering side of a steamer which somehow or other I was going to have to scale. In the case of the *Penn* I went up by a narrow, trembling accommodation ladder, hauling the kit bag after me. Getting aboard was not the end of it either. There was always the problem of getting to your quarters which were invariably in the farthest corner of the ship. I butted my way through troops milling around on the cargo deck, staggered through labyrinthine passageways crowded with more men, came finally to the quarters assigned me and flopped on the first bunk. The thought of that bag and the rest of my gear used to haunt me at times and yet I could never figure out any items which I could do without. At that I was unique among correspondents in that I carried no portable typewriter. Most correspondents travelled even more heavily laden than I.

My other problem, incidentally, was my name. It is a long name and in some respects an odd one since there doesn't seem to be a given name in the whole collection. I remember a perplexed yeoman on the *John Penn* who came up to me and said, "Say, are there three of you guys from *Time* aboard, or what? I got a Duncan, a Norton, and a Taylor."

The name was sometimes a nuisance, like my kit bag, because there were so many times it had to be signed and registered for one thing or another. But like my gear I could never figure out any parts of it which I could drop. The double-barreled last name was inherited—from where I never knew. My father, who is not curious, never knew either. It came to him from his father who was an English artillery colonel, from whom I had also inherited the Duncan. I always figured that if Grandfather Duncan Norton-Taylor could live a busy and useful life dragging all that around behind him, like his long sword, then I could too. I never considered taking the easy way out that Ira Wolfert had. Ira's first name before he changed it was Ivanhoe.

We did not sail immediately. We spent several days in the harbor waiting for the *Penn* to finish loading, watching big flat pontoon barges nose alongside swarming with troops, who scrambled aboard by the landing nets. Jackson and I had to use that method once. We had made several trips back to shore to pick up news and mail, and used to hitch rides out again on whatever kind of craft we could find. One evening we arrived alongside the *Penn* in a landing barge that was filled with a last-minute miscellany of matériel, including tent poles. Instead of putting us off at the gangway, the coxswain went around to the other, cargo-loading side. He said, "Oh, I forgot you fellows. I should have put you off on the other side." I think he was lying in his teeth about forgetting us. A big landing net hung above us. "You can board that way," he said.

From the end of one of the *Penn*'s cargo booms a great 800-pound hook was dropping down upon us, swinging crazily out of control. We ducked wildly until the barge crew captured it. They took a single hitch with a steel cable around a bundle of tent poles and put the hitch over the hook, which jerked the bundle aloft while we flattened against the barge's sides, expecting the poles with their spiked ends to slip through the hitch and come raining down upon us. The boom swung them aboard and they vanished, but the big hook appeared once

109

again, plummeting down from the sky. Jackson and I had had enough. We leaped for the landing net and went panting up, hand over hand, swaying clumsily against the ship's side but so anxious to get out from under that we probably set a record for the climb.

One afternoon we bobbed across the harbor for the last time in a launch with Frank Hewlett of United Press and Henry Keys of the *London Daily Express.* They were going aboard destroyers—Keys as it turned out on my old Can. Joe Driscoll and Jack Mahon had already left by air, but by a roundabout route. With the men already up in Guadalcanal the offensive ought to get adequate coverage. The next morning we sailed.

It required no premonition to know that we were in for something. One of the pieces of news which Jackson and I had picked up ashore was that the Japs had attacked Guadalcanal a few days before, on June 16, with 110 dive and torpedo bombers. Their chief target was the convoy which the other correspondents had gone up on, which was then busy unloading. The enemy had got a hot reception. Ninety-four of their aircraft had been shot down by our fighters and ack-ack. If I had stayed in Guadalcanal I would have seen the show. Missing it was as bad a piece of luck as I ran into.

Obviously the enemy knew that something was brewing. He had observed the increase of traffic between Noumea and Guadalcanal. He had seen the gathering of strength on the island. That strength was not much by Mediterranean standards but it was respectable for this theatre. It represented all the power we could spare from our attenuated Pacific lines, fed out over the thin line north. The step forward which we were contemplating did not look like much either. Even on a large globe it was hardly discernible. But it looked long from where I stood that June. For a lot of American boys it was the longest step of their lives—a step from which they never returned.

The phase of the New Georgia campaign which I finally saw was, as far as I was concerned, a completely unforeseen one. My own involvement in it was even more unexpected. But as we cleared from Noumea I did have the uneasy feeling that I might be heading for that part of the war which was White's 10 per cent, the part which he said was utter terror.

XIV

THE GREY GHOSTS

THERE WAS A KIND OF SUPPRESSED, nervous excitement aboard the *John Penn*. We were moving up.

I remember as a Freshman at Brown University being loaded with my fellows into trucks and carried off over the hills of Rhode Island towards a roadhouse where a banquet was set up which it was our duty to go and eat. Somewhere in other trucks the Sophomores were converging on the same road-house, their idea being to break up our party. None of us wanted the banquet but this was a University tradition which had to be carried out. On one of the bare hills we would all get out and have a fight with the Sophomores. It was a chilly, New England autumn afternoon and we stood shivering in the truck, all wearing our little Freshman monkey caps, secretly wishing that God or the Dean would intervene, scanning each brow of each hill with our hearts in our throats.

The trucks rolled on and the Dean never appeared. There was a fight, a lot of bloody noses and one slight concussion. We ate our banquet, though practically everything including the roadhouse was wrecked.

Five merchantmen and their destroyer screen, which was our convoy, rolled across the Coral Sea toward the rim and the uncertain destinies of several thousand men.

I read Gene Fowler's *Timber Line*, which I found in the ship's library. I re-read my "sugar reports" which I had picked up in Noumea. The various women members of my family— my sister, my mother, my mother-in-law, Peg and my daughters —had written long letters about the multiple, peaceful affairs back home.

From Susan came an almost minute-by-minute résumé of a

111

week end of activities: "On Sunday afternoon," she concluded briskly, "Ray, Billy (her cousins), Joan and I went up to the tennis courts at Maplecrest. It was the first time we had played and we were stinky. Billy and Ray each sent a ball over the fence but Joan and I had no such misfortune. About two-thirds of the time we were going to stay a man beckoned me over to the fence—he was on the outside. He asked me how old we all were. I told him and he said the two boys would have to get off the court because they were not 12. Billy and Ray went home. Joan and I stayed and played. By that time we were pretty good so we played a set. I won it. After that we went home, ate supper, took baths, listened to Fred Allen and then went to bed. We are all well and fine (although Nancy has a cold) and hope you are too. Love, Susan."

The gas stations were dry, Peg wrote, and she was face to face with the problem of taking the train to Maryland, which involved much more than just buying four tickets. "The ODT has ordered milk drivers to deliver every other day but the drivers' union won't let them take two days' milk on one day so our milk consumption is cut in half. Meat is still very hard to get—potatoes are doled out two pounds at a time when there are any." They had celebrated Nancy's fifteenth birthday with a trip to New York. Nancy, who is very serious-minded about some things, wanted to see: the Statue of Liberty, the open-air art exhibit in Washington Square, the Rockefeller Center Museum of Science and Industry. Greatest excitement had been a Girl Scout hike in the reservation. "We were hiking down a bridle path and heard shouts and hoof-beats behind us and went over in the ditch just as a horse tore by with a boy pulling on the reins with all his might. They rounded a curve and we heard a cry for help—and found the child thrown off and the horse gone. His chin was cut open and I stopped the bleeding and found his leg wasn't broken. . . . Your office always asks me if I have any message to add to their cables and I can't think of any except my love."

The *John Penn* was the former American Export liner *Excambion*. With partitions torn out, paint and panelling stripped off to lessen the danger of fires, her first class cabins were now large, barracks-like compartments filled with double-decked

112

bunks. Our room looked like the men's wing of the county jail. There were accommodations for ten men in it and only Jackson, a Lieutenant Colonel Gabbard, a Lieutenant Stansell and I to rattle around. Gabbard was a peppery little Marine with a black, bristling moustache who was going to New Georgia as an observer. Stansell was a onetime Midwest lawyer who expected to be stationed with one of the Navy's shore-based units on Guadalcanal. He used to wish he was back home lighting a cigar and settling down behind the Sunday edition of the *Chicago Tribune.*

All to ourselves we had two wash basins, a toilet and a shower. The shower was magnificent. It had an outlook and it had sociability. The water that flowed from it was a tepid trickle and the drain was choked up so that paint scales and particles of whatever was clogging the pipe floated around your knees before you finished bathing. But unlike most showers, which are a dull communion between you and a cake of soap, this one gave out through a porthole on a vista of the sea, on the dawn coming up, on flying fishes skittering across the waves and the grey transport on your starboard beam waddling alongside with her burden of men for the war. Occasionally one of your cabinmates came in, sat down and chatted with you.

As usual these accommodations were in contrast to the enlisted men's whose packed, dark quarters smelled like a locker room after a basketball game. There were some Marines aboard but most of the troops were infantrymen. They were young, fit-looking, shaven-headed, dressed in green overalls. But for all that they were untried troops who had not yet been under fire. They were not certain where they were being taken or what they would be called upon to do, but they were pretty sure that now, at last, they were going to fight. They tried to disguise it, but they had stage-fright. One baby-faced private from Jersey City told me with peculiar bitterness that they had not shot a gun in months. They had been billeted outside of Noumea, he said, and had done nothing but work on roads. I doubted that they were going into action right away, however. They would probably replace troops who had been training in Guadalcanal. Those troops would perform the first, nasty work of landing on New Georgia, establishing beachheads and cleaning out the Japs. These boys would be shipped up later as a holding force.

Sprawling, sitting tailor-fashion, squatting on the packed lower decks as the hot hours at sea rushed by, the *John Penn*'s cargo of sweating, nervous soldiers dozed, played cards and talked.

There were two basic words in their vocabularies. Both words were obscenities, though the men seemed to have forgotten the original meanings. The words were now merely sharp sounds and were made to do duty as nouns, verbs, and adjectives. Examples in print would look merely nasty and would furthermore be unintelligible because exact meanings depended upon voice tones—not in the subtle, complicated way of Chinese but in the simple, forthright way of dog-talk.

Gabbard and I stood listening to the yapping of a group of boys. "Where do they get it?" the Colonel sputtered. "I'll tell you where they get it—from the sergeants in boot training. They want to sound tough like the sergeants and pretty soon it becomes a habit. They can't open their mouths without being obscene."

The Colonel's theory was probably correct as far as it went. The men thought that obscenity covered their nervousness, and no doubt they infected each other with their habits of speech. But beyond that, the American soldier is a man of limited ideas—with few political notions, no convictions about the war, no consciousness of history, no common aim with his fellow fighting men beyond finishing the business and going home—and therefore a man of limited conversation.

According to officers who have to censor his mail, he displays more ideas when he writes home. His letters first of all express his love and his anxiety about whether his sweetheart will wait for him. The waiting, he promises, will be worth her while. Sometimes he recalls their last moment together with details which make officer-censors' eyes pop.

He talks about himself. He describes his camp, the chow and the movies he has seen. He is O.K., he says, reassuringly. Sometimes he exaggerates the hazards of his experiences in order to paint himself as more of a hero than he is, although on this score he is more apt to be ridiculously casual. If he is married

114

he writes detailed instructions to his wife about household matters, about tending to the small business he left behind, about keeping an eye on the job he has left to which he hopes someday to return.

But the two obscenities do for all the ideas he has to discuss in public and all the attitudes he wants to reveal: boredom, self-assurance and derision.

This has nothing to do with the courage or the doggedness or the ingenuity of the American soldier. It has nothing to do with the American soldier as an individual who confidentially is a homesick, vaguely hopeful and ambitious young man. There were a lot of hopes aboard the rolling, creaking old *John Penn*.

In her crew was a machinist named Karl Kawa. Kawa had a good job with Bell Aircraft in Buffalo; he was married, had saved enough money to buy a plot of land and was saving up to build a house on it when the war came along. Now Kawa was in the Navy. But in his spare time in the *John Penn's* machine shop he was painstakingly making a model of the house he intended to build—after the war. He showed it to me, explaining that it was modernistic. The roof came off so Kawa could look inside.

A lot of other men carried the model of their future in their mind's eye. Considering the hazards they faced, I was astonished to find how sanguine they were. I think in his heart each man believed that he would survive. During war's monotony they had plenty of time to speculate and if they did little thinking about the future of the world and the U.S.A., they thought a good deal about the future of John Jones, and Karl Kawa.

On June 24 the *John Penn* dropped anchor off Guadalcanal under a humid, cloud-smudged sky, the kind of clouds that bombers exploit to hide their approach, diving out of them before ack-ack gunners can get set. But the disaster which the Emperor's air forces had suffered the week before had apparently left them too weak to make a try at our convoy. We unloaded without interruption. Jackson and I saw our gear lowered into a landing barge and went down after it by a landing net. The same kind of big, flat barges which had loaded the men at Noumea crawled out from the shore and took off the silent young soldiers. That was the last time I saw the *John Penn*. She returned to Noumea and thereafter all summer plied back and forth across the Coral Sea. She never received any mention. She was just another one of the grey fat ghosts in the little fleet of merchantmen crawling from horizon to horizon with dark holds packed with food and gear, with companionways clanking under the boots of men—the thousands of men being carried laboriously up the island road to Tokyo. Toward the end of September the *John Penn* finally made a modest headline.

She had arrived at Guadalcanal, the Navy reported, with her usual cargo of troops, who disembarked as we had that morning in June. That night she lay at anchor in the straits when enemy bombers, high in the moonlit sky, appeared above the hump of the misty island. Searchlights on Guadalcanal extended their long fingers for them. Fire spat from the island's upturned cannon mouths. Fighter planes swept aloft to knock the enemy down.

The crew of the *John Penn* watched all this with interest. That was why they did not notice until too late the Jap torpedo plane approaching from another quarter, coming in flat across the waters of the channel. Too late, automatic guns swung and pinned the plane with tracers. The Jap was already making his run, loosing his torpedo. The long fish hit the *John Penn* amidships, must have exploded in her fuel tanks. She burst into fire. She became a mass of flames which spread in a great bright pool, engulfed her and kept on burning long after she sank.

"Landing boats rushed out from the shore to pick up survivors," said the report. "...Casualties among the crew were reported light." This was a miracle if it was true. I have no way of knowing who of her officers and men were saved. I do not know whether Kawa was one of them. I assume his house was lost.

XV

"TERRIBLE" TURNER

REAR ADMIRAL TURNER'S HEADQUARTERS during the preparatory stages of the impending operations, we had been told, was a jungle camp somewhere west of Koli Point. I decided to go there first since the only Navy public relations man on Guadalcanal was with Turner and I wanted to talk to him and get some idea of the plans before I reported it at Admiral Mitscher's headquarters at Henderson Field. When Jackson and I were dumped ashore from the *John Penn* we hitchhiked a ride with some Marine officers in a jeep.

Turner's camp lay at the end of a grey dirt road, marked by a sign on a tree which read, "S.S. Crocodile—Flagship—Amphibious Forces South Pacific." Beyond were screened-in huts roofed with brown, pyramidal tents—the living quarters of Turner and his staff—and Quonset huts which housed the officers' mess and the operations and communications offices. The jungle hung like a lush green backdrop behind. Neither the PRO, Lieutenant (jg) Frank Rounds, nor any of the correspondents were there, nor did anyone know where they had gone. Jackson and I investigated and found their quarters. We could have spotted them without the crude nameplates fastened to the screen doors. The walls were festooned with clothes; cots were unmade; gear, bags, boxes lay in such a jumble it looked as though our colleagues had fled from an earthquake. We moved in among the frightful disorder to get out of the sun. When you are temporarily stymied in the tropics there is only one thing to do: lie down and wait.

This was the nerve center of an offensive that was coming off in less than a week. Little lizards slithered across the screen walls. Onto the paths outside tukeimai trees dripped pale yellow

117

blossoms. Parakeets and cockatoos skittered around the jungle shadows, and the ceaseless buzz of locusts, the quack of bena bena birds and the coo of kura kura pigeons filled the air. Then suddenly the birds would scatter and a bomber, its approach muffled by the jungle, would thunder explosively overhead, so low that it seemed to brush the fronds of the ivory nut palms. Jeeps and staff cars would roar up into the wide, dusty parking space outside the camp and sun-helmeted officers would get out and hurry into one of the huts. Then the camp would subside again into its deceptive quiet and Jackson and I went to sleep.

The crowd never did show up that day. I spent the night there, appropriating the cot which obviously belonged to Bill Shrout. A lot of Bill's familiar gear was piled around it, along with a lot of new gear—shoes, boots, jungle suits—which Bill had acquired in the three weeks that had gone by since I had seen him. The temperature dropped at night and it was cool. Ack-ack guns barked somewhere in the distance, possibly at Jap nuisance raiders flying over by the light of a waning moon.

Around mid-afternoon of the next day most of the correspondents had reappeared. They had been on several wild goose chases—some of them out on a destroyer mission which had come to nothing, some of them up the coast to inspect a cargo ship which had been bombed several days before and beached. Rounds was with them, looking hot and harassed. They were just in time for a press interview which Admiral Turner had promised to hold that afternoon and we filed into the mess-hall.

I had met Turner in Noumea. He was a grey-haired high-domed man with thick black eyebrows. He wore gold-rimmed spectacles and an intense, consecrated look. In Noumea he had had the pallor of sickness, having just recovered from a double-header with dengue fever and malaria. Turner commanded the invasion of Guadalcanal, August 7, 1942, though he has received little credit for it. Lieutenant General Alexander Vandergrift was in command of the Marines ashore, but Turner put them there. He was the Navy's No. 1 amphibious commander.

By reputation Turner was a hard and exacting man, "a mean so-and-so," according to one of his staff officers. Amiable enough in casual conversation, deliberate of speech, he was explosive when roused, profane as a bosun's mate, and on subordinates who failed him as abrasive as a file. He expected much of his men and accepted no excuses. He commanded respect and in some cases reverence.

"Terrible" Turner looked fit enough now. He faced us across a table and gave us an outline of the plan of attack. It was hard to detect in his dispassionate lecture the brutality and terror which he was forecasting. He used gentle, cold phrases like *soften up, move against, clean out,* and waved his big brown hands casually. And yet these military operations, I reflected, were dependent on one basic idea, the infliction upon men of death or the fear of death.

"The main objective is Munda airfield on the island of New Georgia." Turner's finger traced the campaign on a large scale map of the Solomons group.

New Georgia was shaped like the head of a horse and Munda was located at the end of the horse's long nose (see back end-paper map). Under the nose like a feed bag was the smaller island of Rendova. The plan was for the invasion fleet—transports, tank landing ships, and destroyers—to arrive off Rendova in the dawn of June 30 and put troops and artillery on Rendova beach. From there they could shell Munda, across the few miles of water which separated the islands, and the next night, in landing barges, spring onto New Georgia itself at a point under the horse's chin. This would constitute the main drive.

Another force would be carried around the top of the horse head and following a heavy cruiser bombardment of Jap installations would be landed on top of the nose at a place called Rice Anchorage. I paid no particular attention to this part of the plan at the time though I was to become vitally interested in it later.

Lower down, on the neck, there were several clots of enemy troops to clean up and these would be taken care of by separate landings. One force, Turner said, had already gone ashore near Segi to rescue some of our reconnaissance parties and to seize and hold the area. Construction units would be sent into Segi to start work on a fighter strip so that planes could operate from there against the main objective. Other forces would land at Viru Harbor and mop up. Still another force would go into

119

Wickham Anchorage on Vangunu Island, which lies at the base of the horse's neck, so close it looks like a continuation of it.

Bombers meanwhile would carry on attacks against the main Jap concentrations in the northeast in the Buin-Faisi area of Bougainville, so as to pin down enemy air strength. Fighter planes operating from the Russell Islands, and subsequently Segi, would provide fighter cover.

The plan in general was an enveloping operation instead of a frontal attack on the objective, as Guadalcanal had been. We hit the Japs there and scattered them into the jungles and it took months to mop them up. This time we would try to envelop and contain them. That has been the strategy of our South Pacific operations ever since.

It was island-by-island warfare; that was the only course open to us at the time, limited as we were by the lack of shipping. But if the push was successful it would reverse the positions in the Solomons. From fighting a defensive campaign at Guadalcanal we could turn an offensive campaign against the Jap's main base at Bougainville. I cabled my office at the time: "Don't write this off as a minor island hop. In grand strategy this could be the first move in closing in on the Jap's eastern periphery ... to positions where we can hammer them." It was not necessary to be a military analyst to understand this. All you had to do was look at a map.

As it turned out we have hammered at the Japs ever since and since July, 1943, have not once lost the initiative in the Pacific. Armchair strategists have fretted over the slowness of things but they fail to comprehend the distances involved, the problems of logistics; the comparatively limited Munda campaign had been in preparation for close to eight months and in one way or another required virtually every ton of shipping we had in the theatre. Other strategists have criticized the use or non-use of air power. Air experts talk about incalculable deeds which could be done if only air power were properly directed, properly exploited. But only air experts understand this, they say, and I feel humble and embarrassed at my ignorance. All I know is that Munda was bombed and bombed for almost six months, and when the land attack was launched the Japs were still there, dug in, strong and ferocious. In the end howitzers, Garand rifles and hand grenades had to be used to blast them out.

I had a chance to observe Turner in the days before the push started. His hut was only a few yards from the correspondents', and in contrast was neat as a quarterdeck, furnished with a metal cot, a bureau and a crude wooden table on which sat a wire filing basket stacked with papers, a rack of sharpened pencils and a French telephone. We would generally see him sitting there studying something through his gold-rimmed spectacles. He rose punctually at seven and still dressed in pajamas lighted a cigarette, drank the coffee that was brought him, and read the night's accumulation of dispatches. Then, his long, lean figure girdled in a towel, he walked solemnly to a tank shower under a narlie nut tree and economically sprinkled himself. Water was precious at Crocodile.

A parade of visitors began to arrive after breakfast. Terrible Turner was accessible to everyone. He saw ship captains, PT-boat skippers, airmen, listened to reports from all the multiple units that would be employed in the operation. He held endless conferences with his staff, which included a Marine Corps colonel, a Navy captain and an Army major. His gospel, which he asserted and reasserted, was that success depended on the coordination of all forces. He himself was a graduate of Pensacola and wore the Navy's wings on his khaki shirt and had served for a while as executive officer aboard the carrier *Saratoga*. He frequently declared: "You can't separate one military force from the other," which is so obvious you would not think it would have to be stated. And yet the violent advocates of this or that branch of the service occasionally forget it.

Turner's headquarters on the island were temporary. He intended to observe and direct the action from his flagship, the transport *McCawley*, which was better known in the Navy as the "Wacky Mack." After the landing was made the job of choking off the enemy would be in the hands of the commanding general of the Forty-third Infantry Division ashore.

I necessarily spent a good part of the time before the attack at S.S. Crocodile although I didn't sleep there after that first night. There was no room, I properly belonged where I was accredited—Com-Air-Sol—and I was just as happy to get away from the old wives' wrangling that went on under the correspondents' tent roofs. Irritability, I suppose, is bound to crop out in this kind of situation. They were under strain. They were going into action in a few days with a good chance of getting hurt or killed. They had lived too close together during long periods of boredom. They had heard each other's stories. They slept within sound of each other's snores and worked within range of each other's mental processes. They fell over each other's gear and intruded on each other's interviews. They were like a lot of old women all trying to cook in the same kitchen.

In a distant past when I was briefly a newspaper man I had worked on beats where co-operation was beautiful to behold. Stories were pooled and the work of the indolent reporters was thereby cut in half. Some war correspondents in some theatres may work that way but they didn't in the South Pacific, except in isolated cases and those were usually cases of necessity and the result of a truce not an alliance. A man could hardly stare into space without arousing suspicion at Crocodile. If he vanished from the group the others went sniffing excitedly after him: *Where'd he go—what's he up to?* I felt sorry for Frank Rounds. Frank, as the PRO, had to keep the peace, try to see that everyone got an even break, arrange assignments to various areas and ships, find living quarters for everyone, even tidy up the disorder of the correspondents' huts. Frank was the lady who owned the kitchen, as it were.

The correspondents were not altogether to blame for this noisy and confused situation. Uncritical home offices which measured everything by circulation figures wanted good stories and put a premium on exclusive ones. A "good" story was a dramatic and breathless story. A few correspondents threw perspective out the window and wrote of every action into which they happened to be cast as though it were the greatest battle of the war, then sat around and sneered at each other's exaggerations. They jockeyed around to get exclusive stories and when they did crowed over being "the only newspaper writer there." These yeasty fellows kept things in a ferment at Com-Amphib-For-So-Pac.

At Com-Air-Sol I was billeted in a large and practically

122

empty Quonset hut along with Frank Hewlett, Leif Erickson and Osmar White of the *Sydney Telegraph*. Ira was with us for a while but left valiantly to accompany the landing party into Wickham. There were accommodations for twenty-five to thirty men in our hut and except for a few transient officers we had the place all to ourselves. We borrowed Admiral Mitscher's washing machine and did our laundry, spent our evenings at the movies, shared a jeep and got along without any trouble.

Mitscher's headquarters sprawled in the woods beside a river. Our hut was atop a small ridge which overlooked the camp. In front of us was a volley ball court, a horseshoe pitch and a foxhole. Just over the ridge was the movie amphitheatre. The planes from nearby Henderson Field, operating from dawn to dusk, seemed to be taking off from our roof but we soon grew used to them. One night a siren, set up right beside us, literally blasted us out of our cots. We were standing outside the hut blinking up at the starlight before we were even aware of having taken any voluntary action. We hung around nerv-ously, wondering at what juncture we should dive for the foxhole, but nothing happened. The Japs were only doing it to annoy. Somewhere to the northwest they ducked back into the clouds and went home, after setting all the horns on the island to hooting. Another night I had gone to bed early when I heard through my slumber the racket of repeated explosions. I clawed at my mosquito netting, half conscious, only half aware of where I was, and had got clear and was groping under my cot for my tin hat before I realized what the racket was. They were showing a Western at the movies and had just come to the hell-for-leather shootin' climax.

We brushed our teeth and shaved at the single spigot outside our hut. The shower was some two hundred feet away—a wooden platform perched on a steep hillside with a railing around to keep bathers from falling over into the tops of the trees. The officers' privy was on the side of another hill.

Privies in the South Pacific fascinated me. The word is a misnomer for there was nothing privy about them. They were forums where the morning's radio news was read and discussed and strangers met and discovered they had mutual friends back in Greenpoint. Ours at Com-Air-Sol had accommodations for

123

four not counting a curtained-off, *de luxe* compartment reserved for flag officers. I am sure the flag alone in there felt out of it but the Navy is very strict about formalities.

An officer told me that he had grown so accustomed to the sociability that he thought he would have to remodel his bathroom at home to increase the accommodations. The officers' privies were the best, being limited to four or sometimes six— a comfortable number. The enlisted men's were too large for good discussion. I remember one at Tulagi which seated some thirty in two long rows, back to back, and resembled one of those busses which used to carry sightseers around the New York World's Fair.

The architecture of these shelters was universally austere: plainly and simply a green hip roof supported by posts. Screening neither gave one a sense of confinement nor spoiled one's view. It merely kept out the anopheles mosquito. Some of these meeting places, like the one at Com-Air-Sol, stood humbly in the rear of the camp. Some hid modestly on the edge of the jungle. But others stood blithely out in the very middle of the scene. Such was the one at Christmas Island. A great mound of coral sand had been piled up like the base of a monument. On top of this stood the heroic little edifice and there sat the deliberators, aloof, unconcerned, preoccupied. Jap airmen, impressed by the important appearance of these places, occasionally viciously bombed and strafed them. Another convenience provided by the sanitation outfits on Guadalcanal was a pipe driven into the ground at a 45° angle and called, without ostentation, a P-pipe.

Our base at Guadalcanal was a womanless world. There were native women on the island who had taken to the hills when the Japs arrived and had stayed there. But the only white woman who ever appeared was a nurse on one of the hospital planes from Tulagi. She never lingered. They may have women nurses in the hospitals by now—they were talking about it— but I would think the men would be better off without them. It would take only a handful of women to upset the simple and innocent man's world. It is amazing how well men can get along without women. Out of sight, out of mind.

In begged and borrowed jeeps we commuted between Com-

Air-Sol and S.S. Crocodile. Guadalcanal's highways were sometimes four lanes wide, flanked by drainage ditches big enough to swallow up a whole jeep if it was unlucky enough to fall in. The pattern of wide roads, frequent woodland and bare flats around the airfields reminded me of parts of Highway 130 across New Jersey. Modern American roads have a typical, uncompromising air. They are going somewhere. The Seabees had hacked out jungles, Lever Brothers' coconut groves, God's hillsides to lay their highways.

Made of the native soil, clawed up by bulldozers, the roads were easily influenced by the weather, which turned them into a morass of slithery mud, then in a few hours transformed them into beds a foot deep in powdery dust. Traffic left them rutted and scarred. But considering that only a few months before soldiers had to crawl on foot through the jungles carrying supplies on their backs, the highway system was amazing. Patiently the Seabees scraped and smoothed and kept the heavy, incessant military traffic moving. Signboards had even begun to appear: "Highway 26"; "Anyone Shooting Will be Punished Severely"; a mythical boundary between "Koli and Lunga Counties" marked "Courtesy of the Koli Chamber of Commerce." Signs which meant what they said, however, read: "Trucks 20 m.p.h.—Jeeps 25 m.p.h." The Japs had adapted their fighting to the jungles. The Seabees have adapted the jungles.

Where was all the traffic going? Officers dashed back and forth on missions. Trucks hauled supplies from the shore inland to the tent and hut villages in the palm groves and to the airfields. Henderson Field was only one of a number of fields then in operation. Trucks hauled men and matériel back down to the waterfront. Lorries carted bombs to and from ammunition dumps. Oil trucks rolled from motor pool to motor pool carrying gasoline to keep the whole little world moving.

There was no sign of the Japs in the sky or on the sea. We had an alert one afternoon during a press conference at Crocodile and all got in jeeps and rushed down to the shore. Several large tankers in the straits looked like excellent targets for air raiders. A brood of LCI's was bustling nervously off in the direction of Tulagi. But once again the raid failed to develop.

The Japs unquestionably knew that something was up. They were anxious to strike at our concentrations but apparently had neither the strength nor the courage. The slaughter they had suffered on the sixteenth had been a bad jolt for them.

On the morning of the twenty-ninth we went down to Koli Point to see our colleagues embark for the invasion. They were a subdued crowd now, dressed in green overalls, tin helmets, and carrying the minimum of equipment and field rations. I appreciated the solemnity of the occasion and felt no envy. Some of them intended to go ashore with the troops. They had no idea what they were getting into. I left Allan Jackson on a finger pier and drove the jeep slowly along the waterfront. Companies of men dressed in weird, mottled jungle suits waited patiently for orders in the shade of coconut trees. Trucks and jeeps and recon cars carrying men and officers chugged dustily along the beach. Out in the silvery channel waited the ships: the little troop-carrying LCI's which look at a distance like surfaced submarines; sharp, rakish destroyers—I looked for my Can but did not see her—long, high-sided LST's. One of these was inshore with its big square snout resting on the beach and its cavernous mouth open to receive the trucks and tanks which were crawling inside it.

Someone beside the road yelled at me. A small figure in a jungle suit—helmeted, weighted down with canteen, first aid kit, knife, automatic pistol, binoculars, and a huge pack—waved and trotted toward my jeep. It was Gabbard, the Marine Lieutenant Colonel. He was sweating and impatient. He wanted a lift down the road. I wished him good luck when he climbed out again. I lost sight of him among a group of Marines. I drove back. Jackson and the others had gone. Barges filled with men were plying steadily between the ship and the shore. Gabbard, the Lieutenant Colonel carrying his own pack and weapons and hitching rides with war correspondents, was the last man I saw whom I recognized.

Late in the afternoon Terrible Turner and his staff went aboard the flagship *McCawley*, though I did not see them.

That afternoon the force cleared from the channel. Back at Com-Air-Sol we noted that the sky was overcast, which was

126

fortunate for the invaders. I could imagine the force moving northwestward past Savo Island, past the Russells, past Gatukai Island and Vangunu and into Blanche Channel, which lies between the horse's neck of New Georgia and the objective the beach at Rendova.

XVI

END OF THE "WACKY MACK"

I HAD BEEN SOLD A SEAT behind a post, as it turned out, when I was assigned to Com-Air-Sol for the opening of the campaign. It was no one's fault. Rain squalls closed in over the Central Solomons the early morning of the thirtieth, which helped to hide our surface force from the enemy but paralyzed our air operations; our plans to watch the landing on Rendova from the air were wrecked. "I'm sorry, gentlemen," Admiral Mitscher told us sadly, "but I can't control the weather. We're sending just one observation plane up to try to get through but I'm afraid you can't go. It will be too risky and there won't be room."

I was certainly not insisting on my right to run risks but I was disappointed. As a kind of sop, I think, the Admiral told Frank Hewlett and me that we could hop across to Tulagi if we wanted to in his Grumman "duck." Tulagi might be receiving some of the warships of Turner's force and there was the possibility of getting some eyewitness reports.

We were disappointed again. Tulagi Harbor was deserted, and the Port Director expected no warships to arrive that night from anywhere. Another fact also gradually became apparent: we were stranded. The duck had gone off on other business and when we went looking for a boat that might be going back across the channel to Guadalcanal and inquired around at various shore units, we found there was nothing going out of there that night. Frank, who felt the responsibility of getting some kind of story off to his wire service, was especially put out. But we couldn't swim back. We were stuck.

We wandered around the shacks which had once housed the government offices of the British-mandated Solomons. We stared apathetically at a big black and white signboard erected on a jungle hillside.

> *Admiral Halsey says*
> *"Kill Japs, kill Japs*
> KILL MORE JAPS"
> *You will help kill the yellow bastards*
> IF YOU DO YOUR JOB WELL

Of course it wasn't our job as newsmen to kill Japs, but it was our job to report on progress and here we were 180 miles from the action and completely out of touch with it. The sun had set and the harbor was already darkening. We had nothing to eat and no place to sleep. We finally plodded across a beach, past a number of thatched buildings to a tall tower, climbed its steep steps and threw ourselves on the mercy of a Navy lieutenant in shirt sleeves who was sitting at a desk on the tower's top deck. He was Lieutenant Walter Kohler, of Kohler, Wisconsin, and the executive officer of the unit, which was a Navy air base. Kohler rescued us.

The commander of the unit was Lieutenant William Grossett. After Frank and I had been fed we began to take some interest in what was going on in this tucked-away spot.

They were waiting that night for one of their big scout planes to come back. The plane had been sent out to rescue a downed flyer but had not been able to find its man and had stayed out, hopefully continuing the search until after sundown. Now the base was worried about getting the plane safely back into the harbor in the inky darkness amidst the surrounding, crowding mountains. Some of their other seaplanes, displaying red and white lights, were moored out on the water to mark a narrow landing area. It was going to be a ticklish operation which they had never tried before.

We waited. Over the loudspeaker at last came the faint voice of our man, identifying himself and asking for our control tower. In a matter-of-fact voice Grossett gave his instructions to a talker. "Tell him to keep the white lights on his right hand...." The talker relayed the orders into the mike. Everything had to be exactly right or the plane and its crew might crash into a mountain ridge or into the boats and planes moored

129

in the crowded anchorage. From the air the pilot would see nothing but a few tiny lights embroidering the treacherous blackness beneath him. A miscalculation not only in direction but of speed and height would be fatal. Grossett had to be right. From the tower he was actually navigating the plane, whose crew had to understand him perfectly, obey him and maintain their nerve.

Our telephone-radio communication was at first agonizingly confused. There was interference from other stations. The plane's radio man had trouble getting on the proper wave length. There was repeated testing. Finally we heard the flat, casual voice coming over the loud speaker—"Roger, Roger," which meant that they had heard and understood. Now they were coming in.

We stared into the shapeless darkness and strained our ears for the sound of the engines. Suddenly we saw the plane's lights, but coming from an unexpected quarter with what seemed a terrific rush of speed. Grossett spoke sharply. There was a crackling interchange between our talker and the scout. Then we lost the lights again. Warned off, the plane was circling to come in on another angle. Finally the lights came sliding toward us high up over the harbor's blackness. The lights began to dip. We watched. But at the last moment the lights turned upwards and off again and the voice came wistfully over the speaker. The pilot was confused by the arrangement of the improvised landing lights. Grossett spoke again at length. I did not envy him. He had too many lives in his hands. We stood there in the tower following the course of the scout as it groped through the abysmal night between heaven and disaster, with fuel getting lower, trying again and again. Its lights would appear, soar toward us, lift again, circle again, reappear. Then—abruptly the lights swooped in a sharp descent across the blackness, as though tired of the suspense. Radio talk ceased. The pilot was now beyond any more help. In the tower we waited, holding our breaths. Then one by one the string of red landing lights was blotted out by something passing before them and we knew that the plane was down and taxiing safely across the harbor. I heard Grossett swear softly with relief. We had all been standing there so long, so stiff with suspense, that now when we stretched our arms and backs we ached.

Frank and I slept in a shack on top of the mountains in the thickness of Tulagi's green jungles. Early the next morning Kohler put us aboard a crash boat which was making a trip over to Guadalcanal. From Lunga Beach we hurriedly hitched a ride up to Com-Air-Sol.

Marc Andrew Mitscher had a wrinkled-apple face and a gentle, grandfatherly look, though he was only fifty-six. He was one of the Navy's few flag-aviators. He commanded the carrier *Hornet* during Doolittle's raid on Tokyo, and during the long, knock-down, drag-out Battle of Midway. He was not too happy with his shore-based duty. He used to look a little disconsolate and wistful, sitting at his desk in the Dallas hut which was his bridge at Com-Air-Sol. The Admiral was a sailor and yearned for the sea. But that morning he was elated.

His airmen had finally succeeded in getting through the bad weather, which had partially broken in the afternoon of the thirtieth. While Turner's landing was going on Mitscher's planes had taken off from Guadalcanal, had topped off their gas supply at the Russells, and over Rendova had torn the enemy's Solomons air strength to shreds.

Mitscher had worried over what would happen when his air forces went on the offense. He had warned us not to expect the same high ratio of superiority which we had established in the past weeks of fighting over Guadalcanal. Our pilots then had all the advantage, operating over their own bases. When we attacked Munda, he cautioned, the positions would be reversed. He was worried also over the small size of the force at his disposal: some 260 fighters, some 165 torpedo and dive bombers, less than 75 heavy bombers.

Now, in the quiet Operations hut at Com-Air-Sol, men sat at telephones and wrote down the scores. There was handwriting on the wall of the Japanese Empire that morning, writing in long black plumes of smoking Jap planes hurtling earthwards. We had lost 17 planes. The enemy—103!

At a nearby fighter strip an ex-Los Angeles chiropractor, now a flight leader in a P-40 squadron, excitedly told us how he had done it. He waved his hands through the air. He had gotten two Jap dive bombers and a Zero in twenty minutes of combat. "They were making a run on our shipping," he said, "when we made contact. I heard Parker's wild laugh. This Parker was on my wing. The Grummans came in with us on the same level. It was raining and squally. I got to pickin' around. I heard a Grumman say, 'Look out, P-40, there's one saddled onto you.' I poured it on and just pulled away. The Japs took no evasive action except to make turns. I burned one in a right hand turn, then I burned a second. I followed the Zero right down to the water. It was a perfect afternoon. I used up my belly tanks and had just thirty gallons of gas left when I got back."

The air battle was still going on. We rode over to Henderson Field where the dust blown up by props hung like a storm cloud. In the shade of their gull-winged Corsairs sat a squadron of Marine pilots, naked to the waists, dirty with sweat, squinting at the sky which was their world. They were waiting to go up, wrathful because the order hadn't come through. A strike of Dauntless and Avenger bombers took off, rushing after each other across the field. I could see the helmeted pilots and gunners, erect like jacks-in-the-box in their cockpits, looking big-eyed and inquiring in their goggles. In thunder and dust they swept heavenward.

That afternoon we got the story of Turner's landing. Admiral Turner had already come back to his base. Frank Rounds, filthy, unshaven, eyes bloodshot from lack of sleep, dropped in to tell us about it. Almost everything had gone according to schedule.

Frank had been on the *McCawley* with Turner so he had a good report. About 3 A.M., as he remembered it, they arrived off Rendova Beach. There was no visibility at all; the skies wept and the silent men stood on the decks, the rain tat-tatting on their tin hats, waiting for the first light streaks of dawn.

"Around 6:30 the ships began to unload." Over the sides of the *McCawley* the men scrambled carrying guns and gear, dressed in their weird jungle suits, hopping down into the landing craft. It was a twelve-minute run through a narrow channel between coral reefs and palm-crowned islets into the dark beach. From the other ships in the force crawled other landing craft. Crouching in his boat, Frank had seen gun flashes along the beach where some plantation houses squatted underneath an overhanging mountain. Frank and the men with him went over the side into waist-deep water. Fighting between the first troops to land and the Jap garrison was still in progress.

The fighting did not last long. By the time Frank had splashed up onto the narrow beach thirty Jap corpses lay in the sand around the plantation houses and the attack had become a hunt. There had never been more than about sixty enemy troops there and they were caught completely by surprise.

Frank returned to the *McCawley*. "By now landing boats were running back and forth in steady streams," he explained. Troops, ammunition, jeeps, howitzers poured steadily onto the narrow sand strip under Rendova Mountain. The strip was only some twenty feet wide and about a quarter of a mile long and men and machinery soon churned it into a black morass. Out in the harbor our destroyers patrolled. Some of them bombarded Munda on the other side of the narrow strait to pin down enemy batteries which otherwise might have tried to shell us across the strait. From Rendova our newly landed howitzers also started potting Munda. Twice during the rain-drenched morning there were air raid alarms and our ships scattered so as not to be caught like ducks all in one flock. Contacts were made with enemy planes above the clouds and our covering planes engaged in several dogfights. But the anticipated Jap reaction had not materialized by mid-afternoon, when the unloading was finished.

Bill Shrout, who had gone ashore with Frank, was busily photographing Jap corpses. Jack Mahon and other newsmen were worrying about where they were going to sleep that night in the soaking jungle. Then it came.

The *McCawley* was underway, heading for home, when enemy torpedo bombers appeared over Rendova's hump, seemed to slide down the slope and swept out across the water. The ships began belching ack-ack. Our fighter planes were on top of the enemy jabbing at them and many Japs never survived to let go their torpedoes. But some did. Frank said he watched in fascination as their dun-colored machines flew straight into our murderous anti-aircraft fire. The amazing thing to Frank was the slowness with which the planes seemed to move. In between the bark of guns came the yells of gun crews. More of the Japs were down but others came on through a hail of tracers and bursting blobs of black smoke. One was making a run on the *McCawley,* the old "Wacky Mack."

Frank felt rather than heard the explosion. The *McCawley*'s deck amidships bulged and parts of her structure, which a second before had been in their proper places, were now twisted and strewn about. She had taken a torpedo in her engine room. This was not according to schedule, or according to Frank's sense of propriety either.

A destroyer came alongside. Landing nets were quickly strung between the two ships and Turner's staff officers, some of them holding aloft coat hangers from which dangled their uniforms, crawled over this perilous catwalk. Wounded men from the *McCawley*'s engine room, blackened and burned, were helped across. One man fell between the vessels but he grabbed a rope that was thrown to him and was hauled out.

The *McCawley* still floated. There was a possibility of saving her so her own officers and crew stayed aboard and one of the other cargo ships took her in tow. With the crowded destroyer and another destroyer escorting, the ships started for Blanche Channel. The others of the force were already vanishing over the horizon. The destroyers could have run for it too, but they remained, circling the tow. Another wave of Jap bombers was now soaring over Rendova.

The Japs were in and out of the overcast. "I never in my life felt so trapped and helpless and abandoned as I did then standing on the crowded deck of that can," said Frank. He and the others simply stood there with their faces lifted to the grey sky, waiting for the Japs to finish them.

Two bombs plummeted through the low ceiling of clouds, and water and smoke arose. A third bomb landed so close to Frank's small warship that she lurched and rocked and water cascaded over the men on her deck. Over the loudspeaker came a voice: "Plane coming in!" Then, as gunners swung the Oerlikons and as the dual-purpose main battery twitched sky-

134

wards and as Frank and the others stood with gritted teeth, staring up and waiting for the enemy to come diving down on them, the voice on the loudspeaker said calmly: "The plane overhead is ours."

It might have been the Los Angeles chiropractor or one of the other P-40 pilots who were having their perfect afternoon.

The merciful weather wrapped the ships. The sun shone momentarily under the thick clouds and then dropped out of sight beyond Tetipari Island. The rain came again with the abrupt tropic night. Frank and the others stretched out on deck unmindful. Some of them slept. A tug from Guadalcanal crept into Blanche Channel to take over the *McCawley*.

"But she was now in a sinking condition. The rest of her personnel was taken off. Around eight o'clock that night they abandoned her." Scarcely had she been cut loose when the foundering hulk of her shuddered. There was the noise of explosions. Already sinking, she had been caught and torpedoed by an enemy submarine. That was the end of the "Wacky Mack."

"Early the next morning we arrived back in the straits off Guadalcanal."

We went over the next day to interview Admiral Turner. He was justifiably proud of the operation although he apparently anticipated no praise from any quarter for he said sardonically: "If you go in and can't handle the situation, you move too fast. If you go in and encounter no opposition, you move too late." But the main thing was, he had put the men and their supplies ashore without the loss of a single life in transit. The job of crossing the narrow straits to New Georgia and capturing the enemy stronghold was now up to the commander of the Forty-third Infantry Division.

I had an inspiration. I recollected that our cruisers were due to go north and soften the enemy installations on the other side of Munda for the flank landing at Rice Anchorage and I asked Frank Rounds to get me assigned to them. I think I was slightly infected with the fever of battle. I packed my bag, went through the formalities of getting detached from Com-Air-Sol and shook hands with Admiral Mitscher, who wished me luck. The task force's destination was Kula Gulf.

135

XVII

THE *MAIDEN*

I FELT LIGHTHEARTED. I looked forward to this assignment as a kind of climax. When the operation was over I intended to return to Noumea. My office expected me back in New York around the first of August and I wanted to get over to Australia for a look at General Douglas MacArthur's Southwest Pacific command. The cruiser force would probably go south after the bombardment to refuel and this ought to fit into my plans, which were to get air transportation from Noumea to Sydney. By a somewhat circuitous route, I was on my way home.

There were three newsmen on the mission—Allan Jackson, B. J. McQuaid of the *Chicago Daily News,* and I. A destroyer from the force picked us up at Koli Point. Her officers invited us to stay aboard for the show, but I felt that I would be more secure aboard one of the cruisers, which loomed up impressively in Tulagi Harbor. They ferried us over to the cruiser-flagship in a small boat and we climbed up an accommodation ladder—I dragging my kitbag—to report to the task force commander.

He was a beefy, sunburned man with the rank of rear admiral. His executive officer told us that we would have to be assigned to separate ships. "We're pretty crowded," he explained. McQuaid cleared his throat and declared that he thought he should stay aboard the flagship since, in addition to the *Chicago Daily News,* he represented a news syndicate. Allan had spent several weeks on one of the other cruisers, the *Helena,* and would like to go back to her. I got the third cruiser by elimination. Her name cannot be disclosed. But she can more or less appropriately be referred to as the *Maiden.* She was a virgin among all her tough, scarred sisters who made up the rest of the force: the two other cruisers and four lean destroyers.

Allan and I climbed over the flagship's side again and into a launch. A wind was whipping across the harbor and when our small boat tried to put on any speed she dipped her nose into the waves and we all got wet. But a lieutenant urged the coxswain to step on it. "We're pulling out of here in a few minutes." We nuzzled alongside the *Maiden* and I begged for a line which they finally threw me. I tied an end through the grips on my bag, watched them haul it aboard and climbed up after it.

Half an hour later the *Flag,* the *Helena,* the *Maiden* with four destroyers on their flanks steamed out of Tulagi Harbor and headed northwest up the water highway which Pacific veterans call "The Slot." It was the Fourth of July.

Our operations plan was simple. Kula Gulf is a funnel with the coast of Kolombangara forming one side and the coast of New Georgia the other. We were to enter the funnel, rush along the Kolombangara side, bombard Vila, make a U-turn and plaster Bairoko Harbor and Rice Anchorage on the New Georgia side on the way out (see back end-paper map). This maneuver was designed to throw the Japs off balance long enough for a landing force to pour into Rice and establish a beachhead. The greatest danger would be coastal batteries and submarines, with which Kula Gulf was reportedly infested.

As we steamed past Savo Island I felt only a tremor of anxiety. The *Maiden* looked well able to take care of herself. From her long sharp bow to her broad stern, which carried two plane catapults, she bristled with armament. Her main battery in five great turrets consisted of fifteen six-inch guns, capable of throwing out some seven tons of explosives a minute. Eight five-inch rifles, twice as many as the average destroyer's main armament, made up her secondary battery. Twenty- and forty-millimeter automatics sprouted lushly like asparagus along the length of her deck and from towers and elevated platforms. For protection she was girdled with a belt of armor.

The *Maiden*'s designation was a "light cruiser." Actually she was larger than many heavy cruisers. The essential difference was that she mounted lighter guns. The heavies carried eight-inch rifles for their main. She was five times the tonnage of the destroyers bucking along on her flanks. Below decks, where bulkheads were raw and scarred, scraped of paint, she was a honeycomb of passageways and compartments. In her stern was an airplane hangar large enough to accomodate a basketball court.

That afternoon I was more interested in her topsides. I knew from experience that once the night closed down I would be unable to move around the strange, complex structure of her. I would have to pick some spot and stay there. Captain Colin Campbell referred me to the chief engineer, Commander Graham Gill, and as we plowed up The Slot that sultry afternoon Gill showed me around. He took me up to Sky Tower No. 2. "I think you could see pretty well from here," he said, leaning out and scowling fore and aft. We tried the bridge. We climbed up on the machine gun platform above it. "Of course no place topsides has much protection," he said. I think he had read my thoughts. The only protection on the machine gun platform was a waist-high splinter shield of thin steel. Overhead was nothing but the sky. There was no place above deck safe from plunging shell fire, which might do the ship no vital harm but would play havoc with the personnel. For a panicky moment I considered staying below but there was no guarantee that I would be safe there either. Torpedoes might breach her. As formidable as she was, the *Maiden* all at once seemed very naked. She was some 600 feet long with some 60 feet beam, which is a large target. In the end, Gill thought, the machine gun platform would be the best place from which to observe. "I think it will be all right," I said without eagerness. I had the feeling that this was going to be a memorable Fourth of July.

It was still not the Fourth back in the States. But by the time we had begun our attack, the East Coast of America would be in the middle of the morning of a safe and sane Independence Day. My daughters would probably be getting the sail on their small boat for the holiday races at the yacht club. I hoped that Peg had managed the trip to Oxford all right. It was a long time since I had had any mail. There should be an accumulation for me when I got back to Noumea. We steamed in to the grey, curtained, rainy night. I was suddenly, deeply worried about myself.

The cabin they put me in was forward of the wardroom and belonged to Lieutenant Lawrence Gladding Lewis and Ensign

138

James Jarrell Pickle. Pickle had been dispossessed to make room for me. But he assured me that it was all right; he had another place to bunk. We would go to General Quarters so no one would be able to hit the sack until daybreak and then —Pickle was resigned to suffering—he would probably have to stand his regular watch. I found out then that the *Maiden* had been up The Slot the night before hunting an enemy force somewhere north of Munda. Lewis and Pickle showed some strain. But they were looking forward to the party tonight with grim excitement. They told me to help myself to towels, soap, hair tonic, shaving cream or anything else. A steward brought me a life jacket, an anti-flash burn suit and gloves. I had my own helmet. The head of a Saint Bernard dog pasted on a locker drawer looked at me lugubriously. The caption underneath said: "I Will Wait." On another door was the picture of a svelte and bosomy lady in undress. Someone had written under the picture: "Right down your alley."

The *Maiden*'s big wardroom was crowded at evening mess. At our table sat Captain Campbell's executive officer, a chesty, fiery-eyed, bull-voiced little man named John Florance. We had turkey; for dessert, ice cream with chocolate sauce. Florance interceded with the stewards to get me a second dish. I seemed to have a large, morbid appetite. We listened to the evening broadcasts from the West Coast. On the day Kelly Turner had moved onto Rendova, General MacArthur's forces had occupied Trobriand and Woodlark Islands, in accordance with the plans. MacArthur's landing had been unopposed. MacArthur was in command of the Southwest Pacific but the broadcast made it appear that he had actually directed the Rendova landing. The Rendova operation had been Turner's show, and Halsey's. I found out later that MacArthur was less to blame for the confused reporting of the affair than the news broadcasters and the Navy itself; the Navy refused to release the names of its commanders until many days later.

Time dragged by. The stewards had cleared the tables and had lashed tables and chairs together. Men coming into the wardroom from the weather deck reported that it was raining. I decided to wear my raincoat—which covered me down to the ankles—instead of the anti-flash suit. It was time finally to get ready. I strapped the inflated, rubber lifebelt around my waist over my long GI raincoat. An officer had lent me a pair of infra-red goggles which would guard my eyes from gun glare, he said, and my face from flash burns. If I wore them for ten or fifteen minutes before going out on deck I would not have to suffer a period of night blindness. I put them on. Several of the *Maiden*'s officers looked me over and assured me that I was properly dressed and equipped. I decided I was ready at last, donned my helmet and went out.

The glasses did not seem to have done much good because I was blind as a bat. I groped through a jungle of stanchions, felt someone brush past me, grabbed him and asked if he was going up on the bridge. A voice said, "Yes, hang on," and I hung onto his arm, stumbling up the inclined ladder after him. I realized then that the red goggles were almost opaque, designed to be worn only as a protection against light and I took them off, feeling a little foolish and now able to see quite well. It was a black night, filled with a fine, sifting rain. Unescorted I climbed up the ladder to the machine gun platform.

The gunners, dressed in bulky protective clothing, lounged at their stations. They were not expected to take part in the bombardment. They were standing by in case of air attack. I could just make out the snouts of their pom poms vaguely silhouetted against the sky. In the center of the platform was the cool steel mass of the fire control tower, which I felt my way around.

I held onto the shield, with the warm wind in my face. The other ships in our force were invisible. Occasionally the gunners muttered among themselves or a talker passed a routine order in a flat, mechanical voice. There was no other sound but the rush of our wake. I began to wonder what I was doing here.

I thought that I could see a dim shoreline on our starboard side. I was very sure of it. I knew then that we must have changed our course, that the shoreline was the coast of Kolombangara, that we must be turning into the funnel. It was fifteen minutes past midnight by the illuminated dial of my wristwatch. I stuffed cotton into my ears, put the red goggles on and settled my helmet firmly. I remembered the advice a Marine had given me not to buckle the strap. "Leave it loose. If a shell fragment hits your hat and the strap is buckled under your chin you might get your neck broke."

In a moment now we would start bombarding. I think I worried about that more than anything, even more than the enemy's reaction.

We had some warning on the *Maiden*. Ahead of us the shape of a ship leaped into sight, silhouetted against a great cloud of fiery smoke. The *Flag* had opened up and the *Helena*, next in line, was limned in the glow which looked pink through my goggles. Pink were the small bright globes which popped out singly and in clusters and floated toward Kolombangara's blank, sleeping shore. Distant thunder began rolling back across the water. Sixty seconds—then the *Helena*'s shape dissolved in the flash of her own guns and the thunder grew in volume. Bright globes—tracer shells—multiplied and soared across the sky. In photographs the tracers show as streaks. It is a falsification of the camera's. They look more like Christmas tree balls and it is possible to follow them with the eye until they reach the end of their trajectory, where they simply vanish in the pockets of the darkness with no apparent effect. It is incredible how pretty and harmless they look. It was our turn now. My face was stiff. I hung onto the shield, glancing in the direction of our forward turrets, gaping in the direction of the coast.

The *Maiden* suddenly hissed. I learned later that it was the noise of compressed air being blown through her guns to clean out the gasses but I did not know it then and I almost jumped out of my raincoat. I hardly had time to recover from the surprise of it when we exploded.

Even through the protective goggles, the glare of her six-inch guns was like a blow. I instinctively ducked. Sight and sound were merged into one physical concussion that sent me staggering backwards. I was shocked and terrified and angry. The platform seemed to rise under me. I wanted to yell a protest. Possibly I did. No one could have heard me, not even myself. Clouds of smoke filled with fiery particles swept back toward me and I crouched behind the shield. There was a strange, familiar odor which, when I grew more accustomed to it, I tried to identify but could not. There was silence after the

141

detonation, space for me to suck in my breath. I tried to recover myself. But there was no time. The *Maiden* exploded again. We were firing salvos, all fifteen of our six-inch guns simultaneously letting loose. Intervals between were in seconds. I put my fingers up under my helmet and pressed my ears. The cotton plugs were not enough. I leaned my back against the fire control tower, stumbled forward again across the platform, let go my ears and hung onto the shield. The men around me, the pom pom gunners, kept jumping into view like erratic figures in a broken movie film. Their shoulders were hunched, their heads down—then they would vanish, to reappear, to vanish again. I had only one sensation: passionate longing for it all to cease. But it kept on and on, in an interminable delirium. Then there was silence at last, which stretched out. Momentarily it was over.

I learned later that those first salvos had lasted only ten minutes. I learned that at one point an observer in a Catalina somewhere above us reported by radio: "There's a fire on the beach, probably an ammunition dump." But from where I stood I could see nothing. I pulled the goggles off and stared into the darkness, thinking that after all that violence something must be happening somewhere. But for all I could see Kolombangara was the same blank, sleeping shore.

We changed course then, making the U-turn. The night was split open again by fire, and the uproar engulfed us. The *Maiden*'s secondary battery of five-inch guns was bellowing. Not as loud, they were sharper, more violent. In the midst of their dreadful slamming I heard an occasional sharp squeal of a shell whipping across the sky.

The *Maiden* was quiet now. She was fleeing through the flat dark sea toward the open end of the funnel. I seized the moment to climb down the ladder to the bridge below. It was apparent that the men on the bridge were anxious to get out of the Gulf. Sooner or later the enemy would recover from his surprise and react. Suddenly he did. We were bathed in a soft light. It must have been a flare dropped by a Jap float plane somewhere above us. The gun crews yelled. A signalman shouted: "Now they're coming, now we'll get it." But they never did come. We rushed through the area of sinister light while the ack-ack gunners on the decks below stood with their heads back and their faces to the sky, until we had buried ourselves in the darkness again.

On the bridge there was the constant, crowded movement of men, the buzz of orders given and acknowledged, the sound of voices on our TBS as the task force commander directed our movements through the blind night. "Paul from Peter—we have an unidentified surface contact...." "Peter from Paul, I think it is one of our ships...." Then abruptly a sharp voice said without formality: "Hurry—come quick!"

The bridge became an agitated area of dimly discerned, talking men. A figure beside me crouched behind a range finder. Some of them thought the cry was a trick. It was possible that a Jap ship somewhere along the coast was trying to disorganize us, send us groping around the harbor looking for one of our units supposedly in distress in order to give their torpedo bombers time to get up off Vila airfield.

But the plea was authentic. All at once, not far off, on our starboard hand, a cloud of fire and smoke bubbled out, lighted up the unmistakable, rakish shape of an American destroyer. Messages crackled over TBS. It was the destroyer *Strong*. She had been torpedoed. Another can was already picking up survivors.

Our sound gear verified the presence of enemy subs. The big ships had to get out of the funnel. The burning *Strong* was too far away for us to see any of the details of her distress—men rushing about her decks abandoning her and jumping into the Gulf. Her fire flared up to reveal the sharp bow of another vessel, evidently the destroyer which had gone to her aid. Then the flames seemed to die out. The stricken ship was far astern of us now and gradually vanishing. A voice said she was sinking in 100 fathoms of water. I admired the speaker's attention to detail.

As for us, we were crawling warily out of the funnel. The rescue work and any other secondary chores would be left to the cans. The landing force had come in, meanwhile, and off in the darkness was pouring onto the New Georgia coast. We could see nothing of this until from the beach which we had shelled, a good distance astern of us, little bright Christmas tree balls began to loop. A Jap land battery which had survived our

143

bombardment was trying to defend Rice Anchorage. We heard one of our landing force ask for help, he couldn't get in in the face of the fire, he said.

One of our busy destroyers said shortly: "I'll get the sonofabitch," and from a point out in the Gulf pea-sized lights began to flow toward the enemy battery so that for a few minutes the exchange of fire looked like some kind of Times Square sign. I heard the distant banging of their guns. And then the lights ceased to pop from the enemy shore.

Two destroyers which had gone to the aid of the *Strong*'s men reported that they were under torpedo plane attack. I think they were reporting this just as a matter of general interest. The action was taking place miles away from us now. They said they were using ack-ack. We were concerned but we were not waiting around to see the results. The cans announced that they had beaten off the attack. Now they were also heading out of the harbor, they said. Hardly ninety minutes had elapsed since we had opened up. Our whole task force, minus the *Strong*, retired from Kula Gulf.

XVIII

BATTLE OF KULA GULF

I FELT A KIND OF INCREDULITY, now that it was over. Never had there been any sense of contact with the enemy. We had gone in, had blasted away and rushed out and the only evidence of the Japs' presence had been the *Strong,* smoking and sinking, and the one shore battery briefly lobbing shells into the darkness.

Even those had been remote incidents, seemingly of no great consequence. Standing all the time on the edge of catastrophe you cannot do any more than make a note of catastrophe overtaking others. You are too far away to see them actually dying in the water. You have nothing but a few seconds' glimpse of their ship on fire and then it has vanished. You have room for very little of any emotion outside of relief over your own escape.

We steamed at full speed down the New Georgia coast. Before daylight we wanted to be well away from the vicinity of Munda airfield. I stayed on the bridge with my arms hanging over the windscreen, occasionally dropping into a half-sleep. I would have sat on the deck but I was afraid of getting stepped on. The night exhaustedly dragged itself out and dawn lightened the east. Still figures of men standing or sitting at their stations began to emerge. The signs of the violence which we had been through were the empty shell cases strewn on our decks and the dark blotches on the barrels of our guns left by the terrible heat. The other ships in our force became visible, shaking out the white petticoats of their wakes. The morning was grey and blank. On our starboard at last were the friendly Russells.

The wardroom had a good smell of coffee and bacon and cigarettes. We sat around the long tables and reviewed the night's operation. A big, red-headed lieutenant came in, sat down and rubbed his hands over his grapefruit. I asked him how he had enjoyed the night's business and he said "It was all right but it doesn't take the place of a woman." He said I could quote him. Gradually the strained look vanished from men's faces. The starboard watch had to go on and they went out griping about their lousy luck because some of them had had only two or three hours' sleep in the last twenty-four.

I finally shuffled into my cabin. I was glad that I had been through the action but I could not say that I had enjoyed it. I was happy that it was over. I packed some of my things in my kit bag. With luck I might be in Noumea the following night. I stared at myself in the mirror and considered shaving but decided to hell with it and crawled up into Pickle's berth and stretched out. The blower roared dully and the small sounds of the ship under way began to repeat themselves. Footsteps padded along the passageway. We must have been running through the smooth water off Guadalcanal because now there was not the faintest motion. I had a vast sense of relief and security.

About four o'clock in the afternoon I woke. Groggy from sleep and the heat I wrapped myself in a towel and tramped through the wardroom to the showers. An officer was balancing on one leg and carefully drying his toes. Conversationally, I asked him when he thought we would get into Espiritu. He put his foot down. Espiritu?" he said. "Where have you been?"

"Asleep."

"Since about 1500 we've been heading back for Kula Gulf."

Lieutenant (jg) Bill Hewitt, an ex-advertising copy writer from San Francisco, told me later that when he had gone on the inter-ship phone to pass the word to machine gun stations that we were making a 180° turn and were going back to the Gulf there was dead silence. That morning coming out of Kula, when Hewitt had told them that we were retiring, they had piped up: "We really knocked the hell out of 'em, we sure threw it at 'em, sir. How'd you like that, sir?" Now, Hewitt said, he had to keep hollering at them to acknowledge until they finally gulped, "Aye, aye, sir." I knew just how they felt.

We had been ordered back to engage an enemy naval force which was supposed to be coming down from the Shortlands.

146

The Japs were going to try to land reinforcements on Munda. They were headed in that direction. Our reconnaissance planes had reported that they were in considerable strength. We hoped to arrive in Kula Gulf in time to intercept them.

Captain Campbell made a speech. Campbell was a small, soft-spoken man but his voice was loudly amplified over the ship's public address system. He told the crew: "The Tokyo Express is heading south and we hope to engage and destroy it." An uncertain cheer went up from the *Maiden*'s deck, where the men stood listening with sober expressions.

I felt strange and frightened and remote. I had moments of resentment against the Japs. I had moments of desperate hope that something would intervene, that we would get a message that the enemy force had turned tail, for instance. No such message ever came. The hours of daylight flew past and at full speed we galloped back. I unpacked the gear that I would need. Sometime after midnight on another black, rain-wet night, we plowed once again around the head of New Georgia.

I had stationed myself on the navigating bridge within listening range of the TBS with my stomach in knots. The startling part of our contact with the enemy was its suddenness. At 1:30 we were proceeding across the top of Kula Gulf. I had no hint of the enemy's presence. The talk over TBS was blurred and mostly in code which made no sense to me. Then I heard a voice: "Prepare to engage. . . ." To engage what, I could not tell. The *Maiden*'s guns hissed. "Stand by to fire. . . ." There was orderly dark confusion in the crowded wheelhouse. Where I stood on the port wing of the bridge men held their ears and waited. Several officers watched fixedly through night glasses. A talker stood as immobile as a statue, one hand at an earphone, the other at his mouthpiece. Then, once more the dreadful detonation of the main battery struck like a giant fist and I staggered drunkenly around, freshly appalled. Occasionally I was conscious that I was shrivelling up inside my coat, elbows pressing into my sides, head down, knees bent. I straightened up, presently found myself in the same curious, quaking position again. An officer went past me with his hands at his side, bowed like a man walking against a great wind.

147

Instead of the red goggles I wore clear anti-flash glasses so that I would be able to see a little into the darkness. But as much as a glance at the muzzles of our guns left me blinded. The clouds of fire swept over us and I smelled and recognized that odor now. It was the minstrel-show smell of burnt cork—wadding shot from the powder cases. In an interval of quiet when we checked our fire a voice said: "Shift targets."

So far as I could tell our arching tracers had simply disappeared without effect into the night. There had been no reaction from the enemy. I learned later that we had made contact with three, possibly four cruisers, and five destroyers as they were running along the Kolombangara coast, headed out. They had already landed their troops on Munda and were making tracks for home. We had come across the top of the Gulf in a line to intercept them, had plotted their course and speed and had opened up on them before they even suspected our presence. Before they could recover from their enormous surprise we were drenching them with steel.

I stared ahead at our fulminating sisters. The *Flag* leaped into sight, vanished, leaped into sight again, vanished in the spaced bursts of her salvos. But the *Helena* was continuously visible, wreathed in smoke, spurting a solid sheet of white flame while tracers flowed out of her in streams. She seemed to be out of position but I thought nothing of it then. Our forward guns had exploded into action again and I caught the full glare of them and recoiled, ducking blindly across the after part of the bridge to the darkness on the starboard side. I was holding to the rail when I saw the torpedo wake.

It was a thick white finger coming straight at us like a chalk line drawn across a blackboard. On this disengaged side of the bridge there was only one other man at the moment—a signalman who screamed: "Torpedo—torpedo!" But even if anyone had heard him it was too late for the *Maiden* to dodge. My eyes were fixed on the advancing track. The signalman disappeared from beside me. I thought that the *Maiden*'s speed might yet carry her clear of the converging white finger. I was fascinated and leaned out over the rail to watch and saw the wake end abruptly and squarely against the *Maiden*'s side, amidships.

148

Men in the engine room and in repair parties below decks and in sick bay and central station and the control room and in the magazines and handling rooms under dogged-down hatches heard it bump and grate along the *Maiden*'s bottom and thought that their time had come. They told me afterward that I should have thrown myself flat on the deck to escape flying fragments and the possibility of being flung overboard by the concussion. It was then, thinking back, that I felt a little sick and thankful for some Jap's error of workmanship or calculation. The torpedo was a dud.

At the time I had no sense of miraculous escape. I did not even think much about the origin of the torpedo, which must have been fired by a submarine since we had no surface contacts on that side of us. I dismissed it and staggered back to our engaged side. I was a little more concerned all at once with a sound like a steel rod being whipped through the air. In the grey waves a hundred yards away and lighted by our own unholy glare, geysers shot up. We were under enemy shellfire. It occurred to me that I would be safer on the other side of the bridge but I made no move to retreat there. I was beyond fear now. I could see what looked to be, at the distance, small, innocent bonfires burning along the coast of Kolombangara. They were Jap ships which we had kindled somehow with our guns. There was nothing spectacular about them. One fire abruptly went out. Another appeared to fly apart as though someone had kicked a pile of burning leaves. Then it disappeared. It was unbelievable, but these were ships the size of the *Maiden* herself, exploding into flames and bursting apart.

We changed our course obedient to the unhurried radio commands from the *Flag*. "Execute, execute...." Our force had destroyed five ships. We had momentarily lost contact with the others. The survivors, evidently disorganized by the suddenness of our onslaught, had turned and were fleeing back into the funnel of Kula. We turned and must have roughly paralleled their flight. Only a little more than thirty minutes had elapsed since we first opened fire. Then we began slamming away again, this time broad off our starboard beam.

Someone on the bridge said: "Where's the *Flag*?" For a moment then I remembered the stories I had heard of the Battle

149

of Savo Island and I felt panic-stricken at the thought of what might happen in the sixteen-mile-wide mouth of the Gulf if we began milling around blindly, firing at each other. But someone said: "I've got her, sir," and gave the *Flag*'s bearing. Through all the complicated turning and wheeling that night we never lost our station.

Once again we checked our fire. In the chart house a talker was repeating: "One definite target." There was a jumble of sound. I heard him give the range and the bearing: "Three-two-two." Then: "Unload guns." The *Maiden* belched, then the night was still. There were no more targets. The Japs had either fled or been erased completely from the dark, wet world.

But the Admiral on the *Flag* continued to look. "Illuminate to port with star shells, range one-two-four-oh-oh, bearing two-zero-zero." Our after guns spoke and lifted the veil of night astern of us. There was nothing there but the black sea.

Again and again over TBS came the unemotional voice. The *Flag* had an unidentified target now at 5000 yards, 80° relative. A destroyer was investigating. The men in the *Maiden*'s control room reported hearing three heavy vibrations, fifteen minutes later reported a series of explosions. Our four destroyers were ordered to search the Gulf for "the bastards." Time ticked by. I had little idea what was going on, except that now we had straightened out in our course and seemed to be gathering speed. I prayed that we were going home. TBS said: "I smell a skunk." An unidentified target. A destroyer was ordered to illuminate. I sensed all of a sudden that there was something amiss.

On our port hand a beam of light shot across the night, fell upon what might have been the conning tower of a submarine. It was grey and dead and derelict in the rolling sea. The *Flag* asked impatiently: "Who is it? Who is it? Acknowledge." The destroyer said at last: "I am sorry to report, sir, it is Five Zero."

It was the up-ended bow of a ship, not the conning tower of a submarine. It was floating there silently for us to see, the only part of her by which she could be identified. No. 50 was the *Helena*.

150

XIX

McINERNEY'S HEROINES

Tʙꜱ ᴡᴀꜱ ꜱɪʟᴇɴᴛ. Presently the destroyer said that she could
see survivors clinging to rafts. Another destroyer was also standing by. The Admiral gave his orders to the rest of us. He had
to pull out what was left of his investment. The *Flag* and the
Maiden and the two other destroyers would retire. I thought of
Jackson, who had asked specifically to be assigned to the *Helena*.
We stood out to sea, leaving the two cans behind. The cans
always got the dirty work.

We had been on our course for home about twenty minutes,
with TBS muttering and chattering, when a voice said: "Large
ship closing in on us." I learned later that it was the voice of
Captain Francis V. McInerney, commander of our destroyer
squadron, who was aboard one of the cans we had left behind.
"What shall we do?" McInerney asked calmly. There was a
silence. I could imagine the hurried decisions being made
aboard the *Flag*. The Admiral finally said, "Engage the enemy.
We are returning to aid you." The *Maiden* careened in a sharp
turn and a talker beside me said, "Oh, God!"

For McInerney's two cans the night had only begun when
we had started to withdraw. I can only retell their story at
second hand. We in the main force were miles away in the
black morning, with our bellies full of fighting, while their
battle was going on. I got the story the next day from Mc-
Inerney and one of his skippers, Commander William K.
Romoser. It began with the torpedoing of the *Helena*.

The big cruiser had been sunk, unknown to us, in the first
few minutes of the onslaught. Captain John Cecil had got on a
target with his first salvo, had poured out shells like water from

151

a hose, and had already shifted to his third target when his ship ran into torpedo spreads.

The enemy had evidently concentrated on the *Helena*, lighted as she was from stem to stern with continuous fire from her main battery. In the few minutes she was engaged she fired more than 1000 rounds. Enemy destroyers had begun desperately circling her to get her into torpedo range. The *Helena* closed with them and had brought them under fire of her ackack batteries when the first torpedo breached her. Although she was mortally hurt then she continued to blaze away, until two more fish pierced her amidships. She began to break in two. Cecil had no choice but to order her abandoned. He himself finally went over the side into the oil-covered water and just managed to get a handhold on a crowded life raft. He and his men paddled frantically away.

Oil from the *Helena*'s shattered compartments had spewed as high as the bridge, but miraculously there had been no great outbreak of fire. She had floated there blackly, her back broken, her tall stacks awry, her ponderous looking superstructure leaning, her hot guns silent and pointed to the sky. Then her 10,000 tons settled, her stern upended and with a mournful, vast *shushing*, with an awesome grinding and protesting, she disappeared, spreading her black oil on the waves.

The dismembered portion of her bow, with men trapped at their stations inside, had stayed afloat for some time. Then it too disappeared. Covered with the black blood of her, the survivors paddled despairingly around in the empty sea.

Romoser's ship had found the bow. With his searchlight laying a long shaft across the sea Romoser had edged carefully into the area where men were flapping their arms and yelling at him. "In the white light they looked like a school of black fish thrashing around in phosphorescence. They gave us a cheer and I ordered two boats lowered and they began swarming into them. Many of them had knives in their teeth. They were not certain of our identity and they were prepared to fight for their lives if my ship had turned out to be a Jap."

Romoser had scarcely begun fishing them out when he detected enemy vessels coming out of the Gulf. They were evidently survivors of the main engagement who had scuttled off and now, figuring they had our destroyers at a disadvantage, were rushing out to fight. McInerney, on the other destroyer, ordered Romoser to break off and attack and Romoser shouted at the *Helena*'s men, "Take it easy, we'll be back." The two cans swept off into the darkness to engage the enemy, who had begun firing torpedoes. But the Japs evidently lost their courage and ducked back again into the Kula funnel. McInerney told Romoser to return to the *Helena*'s men. The ship McInerney was on, commanded by Lieutenant Commander Andrew J. Hill, would defend him.

Romoser hustled back and fished some 300 more of the *Helena*'s hurt, haggard and thankful men out of the ocean. Then the enemy came out again. McInerney made out at least one of their ships as a large one. It might have been the better part of valor to retire but instead he advised the *Flag* of the situation.

That was when the Admiral had told him to engage and ordered us all back to their assistance.

Romoser, meanwhile, had rushed to Hill's assistance and the two destroyers found themselves in a stalking match. The water around them was streaked with torpedoes and they discharged nine of their own.

There was a sudden detonation, followed by a second one. Romoser opened fire, pouring five-inch shells into the darkness. Hill illuminated with star shells and there in the smoke of her burning guts was a big Japanese cruiser and astern of her a destroyer at which Romoser and Hill slugged away with their main guns. The cruiser had ceased to react. She was dead and sinking. So was the destroyer. There was a third ship but she fled again. McInerney reported to the *Flag:* "We have no more targets."

We heard that message on the *Maiden* and turned thankfully homeward again. The curtain of darkness was beginning to lift along the enemy coast of New Georgia.

Romoser and Hill went back to the *Helena*'s cheering men. "One crowd around a craft was singing 'Happy Days Are Here Again,'" McInerney told me. Romoser and Hill put over more whaleboats and slimy, weary men hauled each other out of the sea. The boats carried them to the destroyers.

153

From the Kolombangara coast the last, nervous Jap once more felt her way. Romoser and Hill broke off to attack again. In the lightening morning they hurled their shells across the sky. The Jap was a destroyer. They poured shells into her with their sharp, yammering five-inch guns. Smoke began to swirl from her and float into the dawn, marking the end at last of the Tokyo Express. Our force had accounted for five Japanese destroyers; three, possibly four, big cruisers. McInerney with his Tin Can Fleet of two stood triumphant in the somber Gulf.

But the sun was coming up over the rim of the Pacific. A lookout reported a submarine periscope. In the sky above Vila airfield, at the far end of the funnel, planes were beginning to circle like roused hornets from their nest. McInerney had to decide then whether to stay and try to recover the rest of the *Helena*'s men, or get out before he was attacked from the air. If he stayed he jeopardized his ships and the survivors they had already taken aboard. He decided to retire.

The captains left their boats with some of their own crews. Among the men they had to abandon was Cecil, who several times had refused to be taken aboard while men around him were still waiting to be rescued. The stubborn and courageous Cecil had remained in the water the whole time, clinging to the edge of a packed raft.

McInerney's cans turned tail. It must have been an agonizing sight for the *Helena*'s unlucky men who were left. But there can be no doubt of the wisdom and necessity of McInerney's choice. His two ships, in the full light of day and jammed with men, steamed at full speed down the New Georgia coast.

The main part of our force crawled into Tulagi Harbor in the middle of a sunny morning. Clouds piled up whitely, roosting on the black shoulders of the mountains. Men on ships at anchor surveyed us curiously. We dropped our hooks. Our two cruisers, we were told, would take over the *Helena*'s survivors from the two overloaded cans, which were somewhere astern of us.

Looking like a couple of Hudson River excursion boats, McInerney's two filthy little heroines finally poked their noses

154

into the anchorage. The men on the *Flag* gave Hill's ship a cheer as she nosed in toward them. Our men were silent at the approach of Romoser's ship. We lined the *Maiden*'s rail, gazing down solemnly on decks piled with empty shell cases, jammed with human cargo. Superstructure, torpedo tubes, gun turrets, decks were smeared with oil from the contact of bodies. Even Romoser's officers and crew were befouled. Most of the *Helena*'s men had scrubbed the oil from their faces. But their eyes were red and inflamed, their hair black and greasy. Some wore bandages. Some were half naked. They looked tragic and numbed. They must have known we were searching among them for friends and they watched our faces with a kind of ironic interest.

I looked for Jackson. I heard someone call my name and saw Allan on the destroyer's bridge taking pictures.

The silent men came aboard over a gangway between our ships. A few had to be supported. There were half a dozen still figures in stretchers who were lifted carefully aboard and taken aft to our sick bay. We gave the *Helena*'s heroes ice cream. The stewards doled it out in cardboard cartons, chocolate and vanilla, and they stood around our decks spooning it into their raw faces.

Jackson had thrown all his clothing away and had borrowed the khakis he was wearing, even the camera he was using. He had lost everything. He had put his camera, money, identification papers, and rolls of film in a ballistic balloon which he carried for just such an emergency. But grabbing for a raft he had lost the balloon. He had floated in the water a good hour, shaken by concussions, watching tracers soar across the sky over him.

He was going back to Guadalcanal, he said. He asked me to give his wife a ring when I got back to San Francisco and tell her that he was all right and climbed shakily down into a boat which had come alongside and was going across the strait with some officers. B. J. McQuaid also left us at Tulagi, in a hurry to file a story on "the most devastating, the most one-sidedly murderous night sea battle of the Pacific war.... Only by a series of fortunate moves did I become the only newspaper writer to participate."

That afternoon our task force sailed south. There was no question now of our returning for another engagement. Our fuel was low and our ammunition was dangerously depleted. Sky and ocean were bright and peaceful. We sat around and listened to the *Helena*'s survivors tell their stories. They were morose and dejected men. Their ship had had an awesome record in the Pacific war. In the Battle of Cape Esperance, the year before, the *Helena* had sunk a destroyer and a cruiser, and had helped to sink two other ships of the Jap force. During the whole long, sanguinary Guadalcanal campaign she had been in the thick of it. She had cruised the Solomons area, pounding Jap shore installations. In the battle of November 12-13, when the *San Francisco* had her bridge blown off, the *Helena* knocked out a Jap cruiser, sank two destroyers, sank the cruiser which had hit the *San Francisco,* and pounded three other enemy ships into pell-mell retreat.

That afternoon we paid her a minor tribute. We stood at respectful attention while a bosun's pipe shrilled aboard the *Maiden.* Aboard the *Flag* they were holding services for one of the *Helena*'s crew, Fireman I. L. Edwards, who had been in the forward fireroom. Badly burned, he had been carried out by two shipmates and had survived the night on a raft in Kula Gulf. But that afternoon he had succumbed. They sewed him in a bag and somewhere off San Cristobal consigned his body to the sea.

I went down to my cabin. The sad eyes of the Saint Bernard followed me around. The half-clad lady swung back and forth on an unsecured locker door. I closed and secured it. Pickle was asleep on the upper berth, flat on his back, his two feet in black socks sticking up like sails. Lewis came in and explained: "Pickle had to give up his other sack to one of the survivors. You can take my berth if you want to. I've got to go on watch." I asked him when we expected to get to Espiritu. "Probably not before morning," he said. "But you ought to stick with us. We'll show you some more action."

"That's what I'm afraid of."

"Well, you're lucky to be going home," he laughed. "Some day I'll see Richmond, Virginia, again—if I'm lucky."

XX

LAND OF PEACE

Nancy wrote: "I'm covered with bright red spots and I have lumps behind my ears. German measles! I'm so mad because the last weeks of school are always the best.... It was good to hear that you'd arrived in Noumea safely from Honolulu. I can't get used to the fact that my very own father is on the opposite side of the world." Another letter dated a week later reported that she had recovered. These were the first letters I had had from Nancy but she had been very busy. The mail which had piled up in Noumea covered several weeks. They had finally gotten off to Oxford but not by car. The government had shut down on all pleasure driving. Peg wrote that the four of them had ridden their bicycles to Newark, "pedalling merrily across Broad St. in the noon traffic" to the Pennsylvania Railway Station. There they checked the bikes and the next day trekked back to Newark by bus, carrying two suitcases, a briefcase full of silverware, three tennis rackets, a violin, a clarinet, and a brown paper bag containing the twins' sailor hats. They had departed for Oxford by train. Nancy, whose luck was out, had sprained her ankle the night before and could "just about hobble." Peg, girls, rackets, musical instruments, baggage, bicycles had finally all arrived on Jack's Point. Did I think I would get back in time to spend part of the summer with them?

I had stayed in Espiritu long enough to get McInerney's and Romoser's stories and had caught a Navy plane going south. Now I intended to stay in Noumea only long enough to be transferred properly to MacArthur's Southwest Pacific command and get air passage to Sydney. The *Helena*'s Captain John Cecil had miraculously appeared one day and under the hawk-eyed chaperonage of a censorship officer told the correspondents how he and the men with him had managed to get ashore on New Georgia late in the afternoon after the battle, although the censorship officer declined to let Cecil reveal how they had been rescued from New Georgia. There was another, later footnote to the *Helena*'s history. More than 100 survivors, carried by the drift, had landed some forty miles north of Kula on the Jap-held island of Vella Lavella and a rescue mission of surface ships had picked them up. A large percentage of the *Helena*'s personnel were finally saved.

In the dawn of Bastille Day I took off in a DC-3 and in mid-afternoon arrived in Sydney, dressed in cotton khakis, chilled by the freezing, ten-hour plane trip, shivering now in Australia's winter, which was like November in New York.

Sydney's hotels were filled up with officers of the U.S. Army's services branches. At the Australia, the Carlton, and the Usher I got the same answer: "Sorry—" Around six o'clock of a blacked-out night the Army billeting office finally located a place for me at the Adam's Tattersall. It was a high-ceilinged, unheated chamber crowded with massive tables and bureaus, a brass bed, and a washstand on which sat a white bowl and pitcher filled to the lip with icy water. The "Gent's Bathroom" was at the end of the dark corridor. On my first night back in a world of non-violence I had looked forward to the voluptuous delights of thick carpets, deep bed, private bath, telephone and service at my fingertips. Later I forgave the Adam's its lack of many modern appurtenances. In the end I was captivated by the arthritic old gaffer who insisted on carrying my kitbag when he showed me to my room and by the cheerful cockney room clerks and the chirruping waitresses bustling around the somber dining room—by the whole porridge and kippers and Yorkshire-pudding air of the Adam's. A few days later I had a chance to move into one of Sydney's more up-to-date hotels but stayed, devoted.

Australia's greatest city bulged at the seams. Everyone had flocked to town to have a crack at wartime wages, so everyone made money but no one got enough to eat, because the farmers had left their fields to come to town too. Butter was rationed

158

at eight ounces a week, a real deprivation for butter-loving Australians. Restaurant diners were on "austerity diets": three courses a meal not to cost more than three shillings for breakfast, four shillings for lunch, five shillings for dinner (about 72 cents).

Clothing rationing was also austere. Four dresses a year used up half of a woman's allowance and she had somehow to make the rest of her coupons stretch over stockings, hats, sweaters, coats, shoes, girdles. In wool-growing Australia there were few woolens for civilians and these were high-priced. Cigarettes were scarce; so were matches, writing paper, tennis balls, lipstick. Petrol was rationed on the basis of essential occupations; drivers got an average of four gallons a month. A few drivers tried burning "shale oil" produced from the country's outcropping shale. But motor experts described it as "bloody rotten muck" which would soon ruin their engines. Some motorists used bulky, rear-end charcoal burners, which were dirty and dangerous and required careful maintenance. Some carried big balloons filled with cooking gas on their car tops and went pup-pupping around looking as though they were driving some kind of amphibious blimp. One balloon had the mileage equivalent of about one gallon of petrol.

The service trades were driven to distraction. Barbers refused to give shaves, massages, shampoos. You were lucky to get a haircut. It took weeks to get spectacles, new heels on your shoes, a set of false teeth. I read in my morning paper that there were more than 8000 plumbing repair jobs in the metropolitan district needing attention. The Master Plumbers Association made the report but had no suggestions.

I talked to Rupert Henderson, general manager of the *Sydney Morning Herald,* and his secretary Mr. Payne about the wartime problems of Australia's publishers. Papers were hard hit by war priorities on shipping space, they said. In over a year Australia had not imported an ounce of newsprint and the stockpile was dwindling. The conscientious *Morning Herald,* determined to maintain its cable news and its coverage of important domestic events, had discarded a thirty-two-page weekly woman's supplement, a twice-weekly sports supplement, a monthly *Home,* a quarterly *Art in Australia;* allowed only

159

four and one-half columns (formerly thirty-three) to Monday morning reporting of the sportive Australians' week-end sports; had jammed five daily columns of social notes down to half a column dealing only with society's war work; and gave two-thirds less space to its advertisers, with a resultant harrowing revenue cut. Publishers were hoping they could squeeze through another year, praying that some ship bottoms would be allotted soon for the transport of Canadian newsprint.

For the little man there was not much fun left. Horse racing, his favorite sport, was cut from three "meetings" a week to Saturdays only, with one raceless Saturday a month. The Australian expended his passion for gambling on patriotic sidewalk lotteries for prizes of ham, bacon, candy. For solace he went to the pub and if he got there early enough he could get green beer or even a jolt of noxious domestic liquor. But green beer and noxious liquor were running short and pubs, trying to stretch their supplies, stayed open only a few hours daily. For excitement the little man and his wife went to the movies, which were packed, and the Royal Theatre, which displayed to capacity audiences such revivals as *White Horse Inn,* or *Maid of the Mountain,* featuring stalwart Theresa Moncrief, who had starred in the same show at its opening twenty-two years before. The old shows were new shows to the new rich. By Broadway standards prices at the Royal were cheap, from 30 cents to a $1.15 top. By American standards most prices were cheap, but not cheap in a country where a good wage for a stenographer was fourteen dollars a week.

Australians still felt warm toward Americans, which I thought was remarkable considering that the novelty of fabulously wealthy American soldiers and sailors had worn off and the dangers of a Japanese invasion had passed—considering also that the American uniformed population was crowding Australians out of their hotels, out of their offices, restaurants, night-clubs, trams, taxis and sometimes even off their streets. But there was mutual toleration and the easygoing Australians were accepting their dilemma with good nature. There was an underlying appreciation of a common aim and a singleness of purpose.

One evening I talked to Joe Young, manager of the Usher

Hotel, who had three dozen American Army officers billeted in his 100-room hotel. "They are worthy sons of worthy sires," he said earnestly. It was the wartime restrictions on his cuisine which depressed him, and he took me upstairs to talk to his headwaiter, who was presiding at a private dinner. My investigation of Sydney's hotel business took a sudden, curious turn. The host at the private dinner, B. E. Pike, a Sydney advertising man, insisted that I join his party.

There was a little more than a score of people, relatives and intimate friends of Mr. and Mrs. Pike, assembled to celebrate the homecoming of young Johnny Pike, who for three and a half years had been in Africa and the Middle East with Freyberg's New Zealanders. They were having cocktails so B. E. Pike said I was just in time. I was placed beside Mrs. Pike, who was heroically calm but plainly moved by the miracle of her son's return. Despite rationing, the Usher had conjured up an elegant dinner. We finished and toasted the King, standing in a solemn circle about the big round table. To a loud piano accompaniment by one of the lady guests we sang the British National Anthem. "And now," said B. E. Pike, "in honor of our guest—the 'Star-Spangled Banner!'" They bravely mumbled and hummed, although a lady in a brown dress and pince-nez glasses knew some of the words and helped me through the high notes—"the rockets red glare, the bombs bursting in air." I felt self-conscious. I also felt, at that moment, the pangs of homesickness.

Speeches followed. They had been carefully planned. The Canadian-born gentleman next to me had notes, at which he kept glancing nervously before he was called upon. We toasted Johnny. We toasted the Maoris. We toasted Freyberg. Johnny's young sister sang a solo in a small, sweet voice. The lady in brown sang some Maori war songs. We went back to the speechmaking and toastmaking. We toasted B. E. Pike and Mrs. Pike. And finally, in the end, a tall, grey-haired man arose and delivered Australia's thanks and appreciation to "our great ally on the other side of the world" and they toasted the United States of America.

I am a bashful and stumbling speechmaker. Responding, I tried to tell them how American boys who loved peace and

161

despised war, who might have been confused as to what they were fighting for, were nevertheless fighting courageously. They knew at least what they did not like and they did not like tyranny. They were showing that they were prepared to die—even if they were not anxious to—in order to wipe out tyranny. I thanked B. E. Pike and his guests for the tribute they had paid my country. I said then that the debt which America owed to her allies was beyond measure, because, but for boys like Johnny who were at it while we were still backing and filling and debating, the world might have been lost. I said I wanted to propose one more toast—to the British Empire.

Afterward we stood in the traditional circle and sang "Auld Lang Syne" and then "God Save the King" again and the "Star-Spangled Banner," and B. E. Pike said to me: "It was certainly a great bit of luck having you pop in, old man," and I told him that it was the greatest bit of luck I had had in Sydney.

Manager Young had gone to bed so I never finished my interview.

I left for Brisbane, by train, rattling up the seacoast in a wooden sleeper and sharing a compartment with Captain George Cullen of the Australian Army Supply Corps. He had seen service in New Guinea. He was bloody well fed up with jungles. He kept watching out the dirty window at the barren, rolling countryside for a sheep because I told him that so far I hadn't seen one in his country. Not a sheep did we see either, between Sydney and Brisbane. The little car tilted and swayed around the curves so that I thought at times I was going to roll out of my upper berth. In the morning a guard brought us hot tea in tumblers and later we stopped for breakfast at a cold, old railway station where everybody piled out and wolfed porridge and eggs and scampered aboard again when a guard swung a big, iron-clappered bell. Early that afternoon our toy engine dragged us into Brisbane.

It looked like an overgrown town in midwest America, except that its park was filled with kangaroos. As in Sydney, offices and hotels were full of Americans. I was billeted in a room at the Belle Vue with one of the few civilians in the hotel —a juggler who was playing at the local theatre. Rebla's one ambition was to get out of town. Lying exhausted by ennui on

162

his iron bed Rebla would moan over "this bloody awful place." Especially, he warned, "daon't get caught 'ere on a Sund'y. I think they even close the churches." Rebla, who was a Londoner, had once played the big time in England and America. He was in Australia when the war broke out and now he was stuck.

I met General MacArthur. It was an off-the-record interview —he had not granted any formal interviews in many months— but he told me nothing which he had not already made plain in deed and communique. I was a little surprised to discover how nearly bald the General was, though he made some effort to disguise the fact. The ribbons which represented his long soldier's career in the service of his country covered his chest above the breast pocket of his khaki tunic. He smoked a pipe ruminatively.

I could only guess what he was thinking. Douglas MacArthur is a strange, proud, remote man. He had come out of Bataan a hero. He had arrived in Australia when the country's morale was at its lowest point, when Australians were talking about letting the whole northern half of their continent go and fighting the Japs from behind the Brisbane Line. The Brisbane Line was a symbol of defeatism and panic. MacArthur rallied them. MacArthur was the symbol of salvation from the U.S.

Now MacArthur found himself juggling balls in a back street while the big show went on around the corner. He was stuck, like Rebla. I doubt if he would take a command in another theatre. I think he was obsessed with the idea of avenging the Philippines, and pleaded therefore that our Pacific offensive should stem primarily from his headquarters. But he could only plead, which to a man like MacArthur was humiliating. Although he was in supreme command of operations in his theatre, he was dependent on the Navy. He could not move without ships to transport his troops, warships to protect them. By the nature of things the Pacific was primarily a naval war and whatever pretentions Douglas MacArthur hugged to himself in his corner, the fact remained that in the whole theatre of the Pacific his role had become subordinate.

He was disappointed and bitter. Behind his handsome, stiff face, in the summer of 1943, he might have been contemplating

163

one way out of his situation—the devious way of politics. In his Public Relations office sat ex-Governor Philip LaFollette, of Wisconsin, a bland and innocent-looking man with the rank of lieutenant colonel, who understood something about politics. But sixty-three-year-old Douglas MacArthur had tasted nothing like the bitterness he would have to taste if his friends ever made him the Republican candidate for President.

I had asked for transportation. The orders had finally come through and I was told to report at midnight at the Brisbane ATC office. It was a raw night. A dozen and a half of us, passengers for America, rode out to the airport in station wagons. We waited. They were having trouble with an engine, and around 4:30 they finally cancelled the flight. We could sleep in the nearby transient officers' barracks, they said. They woke us at 7:30 for mess. In a bright, chill morning we went out to the field again. This time there was only a little waiting. They cancelled the flight almost immediately and told us to come back that night. We spent the afternoon sleeping. At 1:30 in the morning, at last, we got away, with all four engines of an old cargo-carrying Liberator roaring. Besides the crew and the eighteen of us aboard there were some two thousand pounds of mail. We were not burdened by armament. In the tail where a rear gunner usually sits, someone had cynically scribbled on the wall: "What gun?" There were no seats. We crawled into worn, torn sleeping bags and curled around each other on the bare floor. But sleeping was impossible. In a rain-drenched dawn we came down in New Caledonia on the field where, two months before, I had lost my expensive trench coat. I made a hopeful inquiry. No one knew anything about it. To add insult to larceny, while I was eating breakfast an officer picked up my GI raincoat which I had hung up behind me. I ran after him through the rain and the red mud. He was very embarrassed but as he pointed out there were hundreds of thousands of raincoats like mine in the South Pacific and it was easy to make the mistake.

We flew to Tutuila, landed in the afternoon and persuaded an Army truck driver to cart us over the mountain for a weary inspection of romantic Pago Pago. We went back to the airbase and slept a drugged sleep in the crowded transient officers' quarters, in double-tiered bunks. We rose in the darkness, ate breakfast and were off to meet the dawn. In the afternoon we dropped onto Christmas Island with only three engines turning over. We ate and refueled and mechanics tinkered with the same engine which had delayed us in Australia. Some minor trouble had caused Chief Pilot Hassler to feather it while we were still two hours out of Christmas. We were ready to leave at eight in the evening. A corporal asked wistfully: "Are you fellows leaving already? It seems like nobody ever wants to stay here very long."

None of us tried to sleep lying down any more. If we slept at all it was sitting up, leaning against a partially inflated Mae West. At two in the morning we sat down on Hickam Field, dragged our baggage into a hangar and lined up for customs. It was 4:30 before the last man—I—was through and we jolted in a truck over to the barracks, where I slept very badly for a few hours, harassed by mosquitoes. The plane would not leave for San Francisco until that evening. I took my notes out to Pearl Harbor for Commander Waldo Drake's censorship. I rode out to Waikiki Beach. I had a swim, and got my only wound of the war—a scraped chin—trying to body-surf. The Bernie Claytons revived me with a Scotch and soda. I had dinner with them and Bernie drove me wildly back to Hickam Field just in time to climb into the plane.

In the late morning we came out over the edge of a great blanket of clouds which hung over the Pacific and there was San Francisco. I was back from the war.

I called the 12th Naval District PRO to get a plane priority to the East Coast. I registered at the Palace Hotel and telephoned Peg. I looked forward to a night's rest on a large, luxurious bed. But when I got into it I discovered that I could not sleep and put a pillow on the floor and lay on the rug and finally went to sleep all right. Sometime in the cool morning I roused long enough to crawl into the bed again. The PRO woke me early to say that they had the priority. That afternoon I boarded an airliner with reclining seats, hot meals and a stewardess.

We flew over the great raw convulsion of the Rockies. Elkton. ...Cheyenne. Under floodlights we refueled and hopped off

165

again. A land of dark, sleeping peace rolled under us, marked here and there by a sprinkling of lights. We flew into Omaha at daybreak and in a spotless little bungalow adjoining the airport Red Cross ladies served us coffee and doughnuts. They asked us to write our names on the walls, where men of many nationalities on their way across the world had scratched their signatures. It was all the reward the ladies asked. I bought a newspaper. Omaha, 1500 miles from either coast, had had an air raid drill the night before. The mayor was pleased with the way Omaha's citizens had co-operated. We flew off over the hundreds of miles of farms of the Middle West baking in the calm August sun. Kula Gulf, sixteen miles wide at the mouth and not much longer in its funnel shape, was some 7000 miles from Kansas. It was no wonder that Americans had trouble seeing the reality of the war. I had trouble now holding onto the reality of it, with nothing but memory. The newspaper dropped in the big tin mailbox said it was so; and so did the cheery voices over WDAF. But I realized that most men believe and fear only what they can see and the printed and spoken word has far less power to reveal than journalists think. Only a few men have the perspicacity to understand the world's reality. Is there actually a land of some 70,000,000 Japanese who hate us and want to destroy us?

I had seen the beginning of a Pacific offensive. I could understand that in a military sense, in the summer of 1943, we had taken steps which finally committed us. The commitment involved millions of Americans one way or another. The faces of already involved men came back to me—the strained, preoccupied faces of men in battle. I felt some shame. My escape had been so easy. Their escape would be so difficult. For some there would be no escape at all.

I thought of the people to whom I was returning, among whom was an unwillingness to relinquish anything. Strikes were only one expression of the attitude of Americans, insisting on their rights even in wartime. "I'm entitled to this. I have a right to this. I want my share." The loud outcry against labor was good for a cynical laugh. We Americans have an expression: "I'm going to get mine." It had one meaning at home; on dark island beaches, on decks illuminated by sudden explosions it had a very different connotation. We people-with-rights would have something to answer for when the men-without-rights returned.

We landed in Cleveland and changed planes. I thought, the way to victory over Japan lay in co-ordinated operations along several routes: MacArthur's road across the top of the Netherlands East Indies and into Mindanao; the road through Burma and into China's Yunnan Province; Nimitz's road to the Philippines across the Central Pacific, which would sever the enemy's lines to the south, force the enemy's fleet into battle, or press it back, frustrated, into the harbors of Japan. I thought, the great struggle of the Pacific war would not be fought on Japanese soil at all but would be fought in the end on the coast of China. For when we had secured a space there into which we could pour planes and supplies the war would be virtually over and Japan would realize this and defend China's coast to the end. I thought, it would be a terrifying, violent process, but after the European war had ended, would not take nearly as long as some people thought.

I had the conviction also that the busy, peaceful country stretching out under the summer afternoon's sun was committed to an unexpected and prodigious role in Asia's postwar history.

We descended to the tabletop airfield which serves Pittsburgh. We flew over the Shenandoah Valley where Americans once fought to preserve the unity of their troubled nation. We landed at the airport in Washington. The city was oppressive with heat. I telephoned Peg again and she said that they would meet the bus at Easton. The bus was jammed with a week-end crowd going down to Rehoboth and Ocean City. There had been a long drought and the cedars along the highway were pale with dust blown from the cornfields of Talbot County. Wye Mills. Longwoods. It was nighttime and our headlights laid a path along the narrow road which wound around the woods and farms. Easton—Harrison Street. Peg and the girls were standing on the sidewalk in the dim light which fell from the windows of the Red Star bus station.

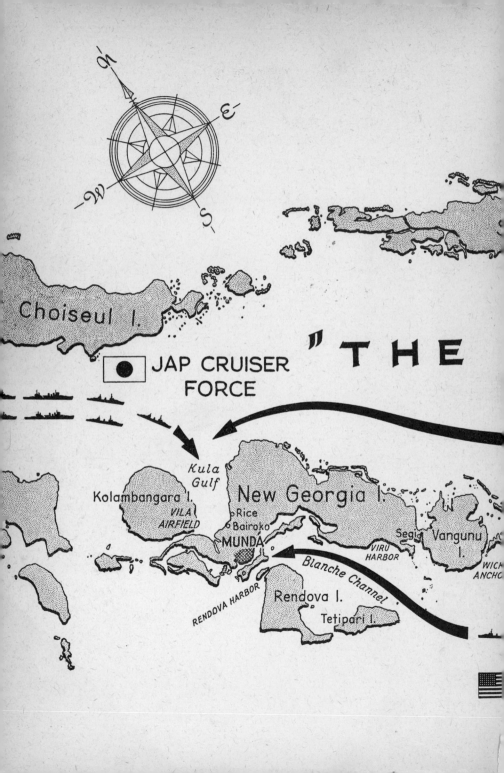

MIDWAY IS.

WITH

Honolulu
Pearl Harbor

SAN FRANCISCO
TO
NOUMEA : 5,440 MI.

CHRISTMAS I.   *EQUATOR*

CANTON I

MARQUESAS IS.

SAMOA IS
Pago Pago
TUTUILA I.

SOCIETY IS.

E   A   N

UNITED STATES
PACIFIC
BASES
AND
THE AUTHOR'S
ROUTE

ZEALAND

WITH MY HEART IN MY MOUTH